CL16

BH

Gloucestershire
COUNTY

12

CARE *of the* DOG

Frank Jackson

The Crowood Press

First published in 2004 by
The Crowood Press Ltd
Ramsbury, Marlborough
Wiltshire SN8 2HR

www.crowood.com

British Library Cataloguing-in-Publication Data
A catalogue record for this book is available from the British Library.

ISBN 1 86126 714 2

Typeset by Jean Cussons Typesetting, Diss, Norfolk

Printed and bound in Great Britain by The Cromwell Press, Trowbridge

Contents

Preface

He toils not, neither does he spin, yet Solomon in all his glory
never lay upon a door-mat all day long, sun-soaked and fly-fed and
fat, while his master worked for the means wherewith to purchase
an idle wag of the Solomonic tail, seasoned with a look of tolerant
recognition.

Ambrose Bierce, *The Devil's Dictionary*

I wanted to write this book for several reasons. I wanted to try to share the enjoyment that my family and I have derived from our interest in and contact with dogs for so many years. I wanted to show that there is a great deal more to owning a dog than feeding it and taking it for a sedate walk each day. I wanted to show that dog ownership can open doors to a wide range of activities and interests. I wanted to show that owning a dog improves health, lengthens the lives of owners, and provides companionship and security. I wanted to try to encourage a more responsible and more rewarding attitude to dog ownership than is currently prevalent. I wanted to try to offer some basic guidance to people who may never previously have owned a dog but who are now thinking of rectifying that omission. This, however, is not a mere care and maintenance manual.

Apart from a brief period during which circumstances dictated otherwise, we have always shared our home with dogs. They have in all sorts of ways enriched our life. They have introduced us to friends all over the world, they have provided interest, enjoyment, a reason for pride, a stimulus to continued learning and the opportunity to write. They have engendered tolerance of and respect for our fellows as well as the other creatures with which we share the planet. Throughout history interest in dogs has inspired great works of literature and of both graphic and sculptural art (though their contribution to music may not be great).

In *Man and the Natural World*, Keith Thomas wrote that,

> today the scale of western European pet keeping is undoubtedly unique in human history. It reflects the tendency of modern men and women to withdraw into their own small family unit for their greatest emotional satisfactions. It has grown rapidly with urbanization; the irony is that constricted, garden-less flats actually encourage pet-ownership. Sterilized, isolated, and usually deprived of contact with other animals, the pet is a creature of its owner's way of life; and the fact that so many people feel it necessary to maintain a dependant animal for the sake of emotional completeness tells us something about the atomistic society in which we live. The spread of pet-keeping among the urban middle classes in the early modern period is thus a development of genuine social, psychological, and indeed commercial importance.

Sadly, the demands imposed by our increasingly urbanized society mean that fewer people enjoy any meaningful contact with species other than our own. This loss of contact breeds intolerance, and none more so than among politicians whose ignorance leads them to believe that contact with dogs does not produce measurable income profit and thus is a source of nuisance. They are wrong on several counts. Even welfare organizations sometimes seem to regard extinction as a contribution to canine welfare. Neither seems to be fully aware of the wide range of tangible benefits that accrue from dog ownership.

The aim of this book is to suggest how dogs deserve to be treated and so to discuss the benefits of dog ownership that, after more than 100,000 years of association with man, have not yet been fully explored. These are largely beneficial to man rather than to dogs. The relationship is not a balanced one. It exists between an insatiable taker and a willing giver. That will always be the case. At least, it will be the case for just so long as political dogma and expediency allow the relationship to continue to exist.

The relationship in this country has survived, indeed, has developed, in spite of wave after wave of efforts, political as well as religious, intended to curtail or even eliminate dog ownership. Efforts to suppress it take many forms and use many means. In recent months we have seen the way in which German politicians have tried to exterminate breeds, invariably foreign and not German breeds, which they deemed to be dangerous. Their campaign precisely followed that which, in a paroxysm of tabloid-inspired hysteria; the British government mounted in 1991, at first against a handful of foreign breeds but eventually against any breed, even aged and toothless Pekingese. In 1991 the British government found an ignominious place in canine history by being the first

anywhere in the world to enact breed-specific, anti-dog legislation in the form of the Dangerous Dogs Act. The original intention was to slaughter all specimens of breeds deemed to be dangerous. Protests by caring owners led to the Act being modified so that it ostensibly applied to only five breeds, two of which had never set foot in Britain and so could not possibly represent any sort of danger. The Act was so badly drafted that even an elderly, toothless Pekinese, the sole companion of an elderly lady, was seized, and deemed to be dangerous and thus slaughtered. The lady soon followed her cherished companion. All sorts, the majority of which had given no cause for alarm and were well-cared-for family pets, mostly mongrels, crossbreeds, Staffordshire Bull Terriers and what were deemed to be Pit Bull Terriers, were slaughtered, often as a result of the evidence provided by RSPCA employees and veterinary surgeons. Subsequent British governments have not seen fit to repeal the Act nor mitigate its effects. A few other countries have, in spite of vociferous protests, sought to follow the example set in Britain: Communist China mounted pogroms against dogs by driving them into electrified fences, a system that earned the applause of at least one British professional social commentator; more recently the Thai and the Chinese governments have proposed that the number of dogs in those countries should be reduced by the simple expedient of persuading people to eat them. The Roman Catholic Church did not go quite so far – in 2003 the Vatican gave its blessing to a proposal, published in *Civilta Cattolica*, that the amount of food eaten by pet animals should be reduced in order to help to feed people who have too little to eat; the Church has not said how unfed dogs should be disposed of. A statement that 'animals don't have rights – these belong to man' supports the proposal. This harks back to the Cartesian philosophy promulgated in the 1630s which argued that, since dogs and other creatures had no souls, they were incapable of suffering, responding only in preordained ways to external stimuli.

Dogs and their owners live among powerful and unscrupulous enemies. Neither dog owners nor politicians appear to realize that about seventeen million British voters share their home with a dog. To offend dog owners, especially when accusations give rise to the offence could, if dog owners were to respond in unison, be an act of political suicide.

This is a book that tries to offer the best and most up-to-date advice on the care and maintenance of the family dog, and, in particular, is for owners who may be embarking on the adventure for the first time or with only distant childhood memories to guide them. The situation is further complicated by the fact that knowledge of canine physiology and behaviour as well as veterinary knowledge are increasing as an accelerating rate, while often ill-advised legal constraints proliferate.

During more than 4,000 human generations, the relationship between man and domestic dogs cannot have failed to become ingrained in both species. Only during the last few years have official and individual attitudes to dog ownership changed. This, on the credit side of the balance, is due to a combination of factors, including social attitudes to ownership, increased freedom of travel, better understanding of behaviour and training, recognition of the potential benefits of dog ownership, a wider range of competitive and social activities, stricter legislation, improved veterinary treatment and the ready availability of many veterinary medicines that until recently were available only and more expensively from veterinary surgeons. On the debit side there remain ingrained political attitudes arising out of ignorance and fear of the unknown.

It would be difficult and probably impossible to find a society anywhere in the world in which domestic dogs do not play a significant part. In the past they provided man with an effective hunting ally, they controlled vermin, acted as guards, acted as children's playthings and provided comfort and warmth. In some parts of the world dogs remain readily available sources of dietary protein. They have been worshipped as gods and honoured as rulers. When man added farming to his hunting skills they protected and herded his livestock. As life became progressively more urban dogs became involved in man's leisure activities, in hunting for sport, in combat and as attractive and entertaining companions. As life became increasingly urbanized dogs came to be used for an ever-widening range of activities and uses. For hundreds of years dogs have been used as guides and to treat sickness, although they have also been blamed for the spread of diseases. They have been used to aid the development of surgical procedures and to test the efficacy and safety of medicinal treatments. These are now being extended. Dogs guide blind people, assist those that are deaf or physically impaired. They are being used to predict the onset of epileptic seizures and to identify cancerous growths. Their presence has been shown to reduce the effects of stress and to reduce blood pressure. The contributions they make to the improved well-being of their owners significantly reduce health service costs. They help to establish meaningful contact with people who are withdrawn and solitary. They provide companionship, interest and a reason for pride, help to establish social contacts and promote exercise. It has been shown that dog owners are less likely to become ill, tend to recover more quickly from illness and live longer than those who have no contact with dogs. They are used to carry messages across hostile territory and to search for illegal and hazardous substances. They are used to search for people lost in hostile terrain and other dangerous situations. Their attractions are used to help to sell everything from cars to insurance, from cosmetics to detergents. Dog ownership is associated with an interlinked series of multi-million pound international industries, ranging from pharmaceutical companies, veterinary surgeons, trainers, food and equipment manufacturers, and book, magazine and stationary publishers. Interest in dogs is a significant source of employment and so contributes to the national economy. Even nowadays the range of their talents and the contributions they make to society have not nearly been exhausted.

Full of years but still full of life.

But in spite of the benefits to individuals and to society at large that flow from dog ownership, those who regard themselves as having some degree of authority often choose to regard dogs as nothing more than a source of danger, pollution and disease. Attitudes derive from ignorance and prejudice, supported by the shrill, uninformed outcry of the tabloid press. Not only are the majority of politicians ignorant of the benefits that derive from dog ownership but seem determined to remain so.

This book has a dual purpose: it seeks to provide information that will enable dog owners to discharge their responsibilities and it seeks to provide a glance through some of the doors that may be opened as a result of owning a dog. If it also manages to

dispel or to provide ammunition that enables owners and others to dispel some of the malevolent myths that surround ownership, then it will have exceeded that which might have been reasonably expected.

Although I have stopped short of providing references to the source of every piece of information that appears here, I have both in order to convey my gratitude and to enable readers to inquire further tried to indicate the majority of my sources. I am grateful also for the help and criticism I have received from my wife and daughter without which I doubt whether my efforts would have taken me beyond this point.

Frank Jackson
2004

1   Meet the Ancestors

Of other dogges...
The first bred of a bytch and a wolfe, in Latine *Lyciscus*.
The second of a bytche and a foxe. In Latine *Lacoena*.
The third of a beare and a bandogge. In Latine *Urcanus*.

Abraham Flemming, *Of Englishe Dogges* (1576)

Prehistory

Theories that domestic dogs derived from several wild canine ancestors, and even from other species, were discredited long ago. Edward Jenner, writing in 1796, was among the first to accept that domestic dogs exclusively derived from wolf ancestors. 'The wolf,' he wrote, 'disarmed of ferocity, is now pillowed in the lady's lap.' Studies of canine mitochondrial DNA have demonstrated that long-accepted estimates of the length of canine domestication, usually set at between 10 and 15,000 years are wide of the mark. It has been shown that dogs have been domesticated for more than 100,000 years and that they derived from a single wolf ancestor, truly a canine Eve.

It pleases man's vanity to regard himself and his ancestors as mighty hunters, veritable Nimrods. The truth may be somewhat more mundane if recently published research is reliable. Nimrod may have not gone out in the morning armed to the teeth in order to kill some fleet-footed creature with which his wife could, with a few roots and herbs that she had gathered, concoct a delicious stew. Homo erectus was walking the earth from about 1.8 to 0.3 million years ago. An hypothesis of James O'Connell, an

anthropologist at the University of Utah (*Journal of Human Evolution*, vol. 43, p. 831), has suggested that early man was more likely to have been a scavenger than a hunter, much as modern day Tanzanian Hadza hunter-gatherers tend to search in likely places for dying animals and carcases. The searches yield scant rewards, but success and failure may represent the difference between life and death. Archaeological searches of similar sites have produced evidence of carcases that have been butchered and of tools capable of carrying out this work, but none of weapons likely to have been used by hunters to kill large or elusive prey. *Homo erectus* males were at least as likely to scavenge for dead or dying animals as to pursue those that were capable of escaping their unwanted attentions or of mounting a counter-offensive. Their efforts would produce little and only occasional edible material, whereas women gatherers would contribute most of the diet required to sustain their group's needs. So much for the mighty Nimrod.

The hypothesis questions man's place as a primary hunter and relegates him to the role of scavenger. In spite of the fact that man would be unique among primates if it could

*So different but with
so many similarities.*

be shown that he was a primary hunter, this is not a position with which all archaeologists are comfortable. Robert Blumenschine, a palaeoanthropologist at Rutgers University, in New Jersey, argues that 'something special did happen with regard to carnivore. The extent to which it shaped human evolution remains in question, but I would think it must have had some strong influence.'

Is it possible that this special event was nothing more that the development of a relationship between early canids and early man that improved the hunting capabilities of both species?

Let us examine the process, if not from the arrival of some 'protoplasmal primordial atomic globule' at least from the time when our ancestors began to walk on their hind legs. They did not make a conscious decision to descend from the trees and walk upright in the savannah. Climatic changes caused the trees to disappear and left our ancestors with no option but to live at ground level where they were far more vulnerable to the attentions of faster, bigger and stronger predators. In order to survive they adopted an upright stance that would enable them to see over the vegetation and so be aware of

the presence of predators. This has since earned them the name of *Homo erectus*, one that served until man decided that he was not only erect but also wise and decided to refer to himself as *Homo sapiens*. Tall, long-limbed, strong creatures, equipped with intelligence and some the ability to co-operate survived, while the Australopithecine, represented by the 3 million-year-old, puny, 1m-tall 'Lucy', found in Hadar in Ethiopia, disappeared. The first evidence of her successor, *Homo erectus*, was found in Java and survived from about 1.8 million years ago to perhaps as recently as 20,000 years ago. During this period our ancestors learned to hunt, make tools, use weapons and construct campsites. Life at ground level also encouraged exploration. Our ancestors also began to take care of sick and weak members of their group, a skill that has not yet been fully mastered.

Is it possible that the altruism inherent in taking care of the sick members of a group might also have extended to other species? Might *Homo erectus* have cared for the young of other species? The possibility exists that wolves would be attracted to the accumulated remains of food around campsites and that they were welcome as scavengers as well as camp guards, as food in times of need, as playthings, as hunting companions and, then as now, as sources of warm clothing. No evidence has yet been found to support the possibility, but absence of evidence should not be regarded as evidence of absence. The possibility needs to be approached from the present by using newly available technology.

In 1997 a group of scientists (Carles Vilá, Peter Savolainen, Jesus E. Maldonado, Isabel R. Amorim, John E. Rice, Rodney L. Honeycutt, Keither A. Crandall, Joakim Lundeberg and Robert K. Wayne, 'Multiple and ancient origins of the domestic dog') pooled their resources to study 140 dogs representing sixty-seven breeds and 162 wolves from twenty-seven different localities throughout the world. Coyotes and three jackal species were also examined. The mitochondrial DNA control region sequences examined revealed that domestic dogs diverged from jackals to a far greater extent than they diverged from wolves. This suggested that wolves rather than jackals were the ancestors of domestic dogs. The sequence divergence also suggested that domestic dogs originated more than 100,000 years ago and possibly as long ago as 135,000 years – well within the time range occupied by *Homo erectus*. The evidence effectively destroyed hypotheses based on archaeological evidence that domestic dogs came into being about 14,000 years ago and raised the possibility that the association between man and wolves arose about 400,000 years ago, one that is supported by the archaeology.

Throughout the last 100,000 years domestic dogs have been subjected to a continual process of selection by man, as well as episodes of back-crossing with wolves. The process is unlikely ever to come to an end, it will continue for just as long as man and dogs continue to enjoy their unique relationship. Breeders will continue to modify the

appearance, behaviour and health of existing breeds and will, from time to time, produce new ones, most of which will quickly disappear without trace. New uses will be found for dogs and their ability to perform their existing functions will be improved.

A great many dog breeders indulge themselves by trying, using whatever evidence may be available and more than a pinch or two of imagination, to prove, if only to their own satisfaction, that their particular breed is of ancient origin and probably the progenitor of many others. Even people who regard themselves as scientists may become involved in the harmless if pointless game. The identification of breeds from the past can only rely on pictorial depictions. These are not always reliable and fall a long way short of indicating when existing breeds might have come into being. Certainly there are a number of existing breeds that are very similar to those that appear on Assyrian, Egyptian, Greek, Chinese and Peruvian monuments, as well as sculptures from these and other civilizations. However, since the pictorial record has a beginning and an end but seldom anything in the middle to provide evidence of a continuous existence, the possibility must be considered that some modern breeds may have been produced to resemble those from antiquity. If they were works of art in the strictest sense they would be regarded as forgeries or at best copies. To use them in order to provide evidence for their supposed ancient origin produces a hypothesis that is not susceptible to proof.

The analysis of mitochondrial samples by Dr Robert K. Wayne at the University College of Los Angeles published in 1998 suggests that domestic dogs became differentiated from their wolf ancestors over 100,000 years ago, by which time *Homo erectus* had disappeared from the scene and been replaced first by *Homo neanderthalensis* and then, about 100,000 years ago, by

Homo sapiens. It is on this point that scientists differ on what they regard as the truth. Dr Peter Savolainen, of the Stockholm Royal Institute of Technology, believes that a history of that length for domestic dogs is implausible. He argues that the analysis of DNA samples taken from wolves and domestic dogs demonstrates a 40,000-year history if dogs descended from a single wolf, and about 15,000 years ago if a number of wolves were involved as the precursors of domestic dogs. He further claims that there is no archaeological evidence to support Wayne's case. Carlos Vilá and his colleagues further suggest that the morphological changes that differentiate domestic dogs from wolves took place around 10 to 15,000 years ago when man abandoned life as a nomadic hunter-gatherer in favour of life as a settled farmer. Earlier experts had suggested the relationship between man and dog came into being only about 14,000 years ago. Part of the argument is based on the fact that before this date few canine remains had been found alongside man's remains. In fact, conclusive evidence exists which demonstrates a far longer relationship. This is to be found in numerous cave paintings dating from the late palaeolithic period as in the Ardèche gorges in France, which date from about 31,000 years ago and illustrate the use of dogs during man's hunting expeditions. By this time the relationship was obviously well established and sufficiently important for man to record it in his paintings.

Archaeological excavations and subsequent studies have sometimes been lax in their treatment of canine remains. Among the exceptions is the grave of a woman whose left hand was resting on a small dog, found in Ein Mallaha, Israel. The find dates from about 12,000 years ago and so is currently among the first pieces of tangible evidence of a relationship between man and

Fox terriers were once one of the most popular breeds in Britain but are now neglected.

dogs. Another is the canine skeleton found at Starr Carr, near Scarborough. This was dated from about 9,500 years ago and another was found in the Jaguar Cave, Idaho that proves Native Americans had domestic dogs about 3,500 years ago. The Windmill Hill excavations, near Avebury in Wiltshire, uncovered from a ditch a 5,000-year-old skeleton of a dog that, in size and shape, closely resembled a Greyhound. It is especially interesting in that its tail was long and straight, not the curled, Spitz-like tail of many primitive domestic breeds. The skull was narrow, the stop pronounced and the muzzle comparatively short; there was a well-marked sagittal crest, suggesting great biting power, and the nasal openings were flared, after the manner of a scent hound.

The feet were large and splayed and the hindquarters well turned, again in contrast with many primitive breeds. Wear on the teeth suggested that this was a young dog which had lived on a good diet but which had been used for some activity which exposed it to injury. It might have been a hound used to hunt boar or some other quarry and have lost teeth in combat, or it might have been a pastoral breed used for herding and guarding flocks and been injured by a kick from a cow or in a fight with some predator. The skull of a smaller but otherwise identical dog to the more complete skeleton was also found nearby and may well have been a bitch of the same breed. Also found was a tooth from a dog very much larger than both and part of a skull from a much smaller but adult dog. It appears that the neolithic tribe that lived at Windmill Hill may well have had three, and possibly four, different breeds, each with its own distinct characteristics.

The association between man and wild canids dates from about 100,000 years ago and by about 15,000 years ago man had begun to develop the types of domestic dog appropriate to his needs. That process has now given rise to about 5,000 different breeds throughout the world and new ones continue to be produced either in the hope that they will be better than those that already exists or in the hope of profit.

Population

Britain is often presented of a nation of dog lovers with a far higher population of them than in other countries. In fact, dog ownership and regard for dogs is a world-wide phenomenon and, as far as population is concerned, Britain is a long way from the top of the European league. Surveys carried out during the early 1980s show that the percentage of British households that con- tain at least one dog is lower than in Belgium, Denmark, France, the Netherlands, as well as in Australia, Canada and the USA. In 2002 the Petfoods Manufacturers Association (PFMA) annual survey estimated that there were about 4.8 million dogs in the United Kingdom, of which about 59 per cent were pedigree. The dog population had fallen from its peak of 7.4 million achieved in 1989, and the PFMA ascribed this to more people living alone and to an increase in the number of households in which all the adults were employed. Other reasons include generally hostile and often inaccurate media attention and campaigns by welfare agencies to make licensing and registration compulsory, threats by government of punitive legislation and the hostile and occasionally illegal actions of some local authorities. It is a salutary thought that these various agencies appear to ignore or be unaware of the economic benefits that accrue not least of which is the VAT produced by the annual sale of £1.5 billions worth of pet food.

Percentage of Households Containing One or More Dogs

Country	Percentage
Australia	39
Austria	17
Belgium	30
Canada	33
Denmark	26
Finland	22
France	35
Germany	13
Italy	20
Japan	13
Netherlands	26
Norway	16
Sweden	20
Switzerland	14
United Kingdom	23
USA	42

2 Making a Choice

If you pick up a starving dog and make him prosperous, he will not bite you. This is the principal difference between a man and a dog.

Josh Billings

There are about 5,000 breeds of dog scattered throughout the world, but choice in Britain is effectively limited to the 200 or so recognized by the Kennel Club, a handful of unrecognized breeds, to very few cross-breeds and to mongrels. Elsewhere the choice is appreciably wider. Breeds range from old to new, from utilitarian to purely decorative, from small to very large indeed, from fast to the lethargic. Owners are attracted to a particular breed or to an individual dog because its appearance and character appeals to them. The dog's appearance may derive from years, perhaps hundreds of years of selective breeding that have combined function with aesthetic appeal. Appreciation of appearance is not, as we are sometimes asked to believe, confined to dogs destined for the show bench. The beauty of dogs has been celebrated in descriptions and depictions in literature and graphic art down the ages.

Pedigree, Cross-Breed or Mongrel

A pedigree dog may be defined as one whose parents are of the same breed, usually but not invariably, a breed recognized by the Kennel Club. A cross-breed is the product of a mating between two pedigree dogs of different breeds. A mongrel is a dog of unknown parentage. A superficial resemblance to a breed does not make it a pedigree or even a cross-breed. Nevertheless, veterinarians and welfare agencies have a propensity, whether out of ignorance or an antipathy to mongrels, to regard the terms as interchangeable.

From time to time the idea surfaces that there is money to be made by breeding and selling cross-bred and mongrel dogs. The 200 or so breeds available in this country are deemed not to provide sufficient variety to satisfy every taste and need. In the past the idea has even received some support from the veterinary profession and is welcomed by those who regard inbreeding as a dangerous and damaging practice. It is sometimes argued that mongrels are more intelligent, hardier, friendlier and in every way more desirable than their pedigree counterparts. If this were true, they would dominate every activity, except showing, in which dogs are engaged. In fact, very few mongrels are employed in activities that require outstanding physical or mental qualities. Compared with their numbers in the dog population as whole, far more mongrels find their way into welfare kennels than do pedigree dogs. This may be a product of an 'easy come, easy go' philosophy, but may also result from a

Do dogs have any awareness of the disparity in size between different breeds?

failure to fulfil their owners' needs or expectations.

The production of cross-bred dogs relies on the existence of a pool of pedigree dogs. Cross-bred dogs are all F1 – first generation – hybrids, which, if mated together, produce a varied collection of F2 hybrids based on a dangerously small gene pool and probably not exhibiting the desirable qualities of their parents. The step from cross-bred to breed is an enormous one, which has seldom been achieved within the lifetime of an individual breeder. It is entirely possible that cross-bred dogs might carry fewer hereditary defects than do their pure-bred counterparts. But, since, it is unlikely that parents will be subjected to such screening as already exists, it is equally possible that they may carry an even greater load of inherited problems –

perhaps even a load as great as that carried by our own species.

Pedigree dogs have a number of advantages. Their adult appearance, size and, within limits, temperaments and behavioural characteristics, even their expected life spans, are predictable. Buyers know, more or less, what they are getting, which is certainly not the case with cross-bred dogs. Of course, many, if not most, cross-bred puppies will be very attractive, but what will they look like as adults? Perhaps nothing so much as cross between a bunch of keys and a doormat, but then the same might be said of the breed which has kept me and mine in thrall these last forty and more years. It is perhaps significant that the marketing of cross-bred puppies tends to rely heavily on their alleged pedigree parents. Even the welfare agencies seek to make a discarded puppy or adult more attractive by suggesting that it is a cross between certain breeds. In reality, they seldom have the faintest idea what the parentage might be. They would be on shaky ground legally if their claims were challenged in the courts. Of course, without a sea change in its ethos the Kennel Club will not register these so-called 'designer dogs', which is not to say that some other organization will not provide alternative registration facilities. Whether these alternative registries will have any real value is open to considerable doubt.

Gratius explored something close to the concept when he compared British dogs with the Thessalian dogs, from Azorus and Pherae, with the wily Acarnian, remarked upon for its silent stealth, and with the Aetolian stock that he condemned for its pointless barking. He then went on to explain how, by means of judicious crosses between dogs from several places, the lively intelligence of Umbrian dogs could counteract the slow wits of those from Gaul, the Hyracians could impart courage into Gelonoan dogs and the Calydonian have its tendency to unnecessary barking corrected. 'So', said Gratius, 'do we cull something from every flower, while kindly nature seconds our efforts.'

Gratius lived at a time when breeds were still being developed, but it is difficult to see why there now is a perceived need for 'designer dogs'. To make money is, of course, a prime motivation for breeding and selling them, but neither would happen unless significant numbers of the puppy-buying public were persuaded that cross-breeds are preferable to pedigree dogs.

All but a few pedigree breeds to be found in Britain are recognized by the Kennel Club. Prejudice often gives rise to tabloid reports that suggest that pedigree dogs lack intelligence, are temperamentally suspect, are delicate and suffer from a host of genetically-transmitted diseases. In fact, our own species carries far more of these than does any breed of dog.

No species, domestic or wild, can be said to be totally free of inherited abnormalities. About 4,000 such have been identified in our own species and fewer than 400 in domestic dogs. Since there are no schemes to monitor the genetic well-being of mongrels and cross-breeds, it is impossible to say whether they are genetically healthier than pedigree dogs which are subjected to considerable scrutiny and which benefit from research funded by the Kennel Club as well as by other concerned organizations.

Although here and in other works that explore the process of making a choice of dog it is assumed that a rational process will be involved, in fact, the business of selecting a breed is no more rational than that of choosing a spouse: all manner of considerations impinge on the decision and not all are either rational or logical.

If the intention is to become involved in some competitive or sporting activity, the

The only difference between a Standard and a Toy Poodle is one of size.

range of choice will be narrowed down to a few breeds that excel in the particular activity. All dogs can and should be taught to be obedient but only a handful can hope to succeed in high-class competition. Of the twenty-nine bitches and twenty-five dogs that won their way to the Cruft's obedience championship in 2003, thirty-five were Working Sheepdogs, sixteen were Border

Collies, two were German Shepherd Dogs (Alsatians) and one was a Golden Retriever. It is not just horses that are suited by different courses.

For potential owners who expect nothing more than companionship the choice may rest on size, coat type, physical characteristics, previous contact and on both the initial and the on-going cost.

Recognized Breeds

Unless prospective owners already have a breed in mind, they are faced with an almost bewildering range of choice. Apart from visiting a large dog show or one of the Kennel Club's Discover Dogs promotions, at which most recognized breeds are to be seen, the best place to start might be the Breed Standards published by the Kennel Club. A good and reliable book that examines many breeds might help to take the process a step further. As the range of choice narrows, books written by genuine experts with a proven knowledge of a breed will begin to fill in the gaps until a decision is made.

Giant Breeds

Breeds that weigh more than 40kg (about 90lb) should be regarded as giant breeds. These are expensive to feed and to rear well and so good specimens are neither cheap nor easy to acquire. Such breeds tend to have rather short lives, some as little as five years or less, some are prone to skeleton defects, some have profuse coats that demand frequent grooming, and their size limits the welcome they may receive in dog-unfriendly situations. Most of these breeds have good temperaments but can be very effective as guards.

Large Breeds

Large breeds are somewhat easier to accommodate in the average home than the giant breeds. Some, however, have a superabundance of energy that can pose a threat to delicate items in the home, while their exuberant friendliness may be a source of concern to small and fragile members of the family.

Middle-Sized Breeds

The breeds that might find a place under this admittedly imprecise heading could be said to be of a size that can be accommodated in most homes, will enjoy extensive exercise or be content on the hearth rug. Most medium-sized dogs are robust and free of the problems associated with the extremes of size.

Small Breeds

This category includes most of the terrier breeds. Those worthy of the name have the ability to get over, under or through virtually any obstacle if they decide to go in search of 'love and beauty' or to indulge in a sporting expedition.

Toy Breeds

Breeds that weigh less than about 5kg (11lb).

Pedigree

A pedigree is no more than a family tree, a record of the names of a dog's parents, grandparents, great-grandparents and so on through the generations. Most breeders provide a three- or four-generation pedigree for owners and some provide a five-generation one. Owners may enjoy extending the pedigree through still more generations and it is perfectly possible to make use of the Kennel Club library or archival material held and sometimes published by breed clubs to extend a pedigree through the last hundred or more years, about forty generations and several hundred individuals. Some owners

---

Popularity

The population of dogs in Britain peaked in about 1990 at about 7.4 million, and fell during the next decade, as described in Chapter 1. But at the same time as the total dog population was in decline, the number of registrations processed by the Kennel Club rose steadily.

United Kingdom Dog Population and Kennel Club Registrations

Year	UK Totals (M)*	Registrations			
1984	6.1	184,043	1994	6.65	246,707
1985	6.3	198,290	1995	6.55	264,091
1986	6.9	189,416	1996	6.9	273,341
1987	6.8	181,436	1997	6.1	268,940
1998	7.3	166,550	1998	6.9	258,864
1989	7.4	283,915	1999	6.7	242,382
1990	7.4	270,769	2000	6.4	247,299
1991	7.3	252,524	2001	–	220,799
1992	7.25	240,157	2002	–	226,318
1993	6.9	235,893			

* Note: annual pet ownership surveys

---

may find the exercise enjoyable, but unless it reveals information about a particular dog it is of no particular value.

Prospective owners should learn to 'read' a pedigree in order to get some idea about the degree of inbreeding involved in their dog's ancestry. Although most breeds were created by close inbreeding allied to stringent process of selection, by both their breeders and their ability to survive disease as well as Spartan conditions, it has recently come to be appreciated that inbreeding spreads inherited conditions both good and bad, reduces the ability to withstand infections, increases infertility and shortens the lifespan. (*See* Chapter 4, Inbreeding.) Anyone buying a puppy should beware of any that are the product of a closer relationship than would be allowed in our own species. But it must, however, be stressed that the absence of a pedigree, in mongrels for example, does not necessarily mean that a dog is not inbred: dogs that spend their lives wandering the streets do not have the social hierarchy that prevents inbreeding in wild canids. A dominant male will mate most of the bitches in his territory. In the course of time, at least some of his daughters will be wandering the streets and their father will mate some of these. When he loses his dominant position he is likely to be replaced by one of his sons who may then mate his mother, his sisters and eventually his own daughters. Inbreeding is probably rife in a mongrel population. One way to avoid inbreeding is to acquire a genuine cross-bred dog, the product of a mating between two dogs of known pedigree and of different breeds whose pedigrees do not contain the same dog.

Unrecognized Breeds

In addition, there are a number of well-established breeds of British origin that are not recognized by the Kennel Club. Each has its own dedicated band of supporters. They include Lurchers, Patterdale or Fell Terriers, Jack Russell Terriers and a few created by individuals in a bid for immortality or commercial advantage. These include Lucas and Plummer Terriers, Honeywell Spaniels, and something called a Spocker,

Average Weights of Kennel Club Recognized Breeds

Each breed contains individuals with a range of weights, but all exist within a range that is larger for the giant breeds than for the toy breeds. Bitches tend to be smaller than dogs. Most of the Breed Standards make provision for an acceptable range of sizes and there are individuals that will be appreciably bigger or smaller than what is regarded as the ideal range. What follows then should be taken as no more than a guide that may not be sufficiently accurate to provide reliable information about appropriate medicine doses.

The information is derived from those Kennel Club and American Kennel Club breed standards that indicate ideal weights. Improved standards of care have a tendency to increase the size of all breeds. In many the males are appreciably larger than females, in a few the females are the larger.

Average Breed Weights

Breed	Average weight kg (lb)	Breed	Average weight kg (lb)
Affenpinscher	3.5 (7.7)	Bouvier des Flandres	40.0 (88)
Afghan Hound	22.5 (49.5)	Boxer	29.0 (64)
Airedale Terrier	21.5 (47.3)	Bracco Italiano	32.5 (71.5)
Akbash	50.0 (110)	Briard	34.0 (75)
Akita	16.5 (36.3)	Brittany	16.0 (35.2)
Alaskan Malamute	36.25 (79.8)	Bull Terrier	26.0 (57.2)
Alpine Dachsbracke	16.0 (35.2)	Bull Terrier, Miniature	9.0 (20)
American Cocker Spaniel	11.25 (24.8)	Bulldog	23.5 (51.7)
Anatolian Shepherd Dog	52.25 (115)	Bullmastiff	52.0 (114.4)
Australian Cattle Dog	17.00 (37.4)	Cairn Terrier	6.0 (13.2)
Australian Shepherd Dog	–	Canaan Dog	20.5 (45)
Australian Silky Terrier	4.0 (9)	Canadian Eskimo Dog	37.5 (82.5)
Australian Terrier	5.75 (12.7)	Cavalier King Charles Spaniel	6.25 (13.8)
Basenji	10.5 (23)	Cesky Terrier	6.75 (14.9)
Basset Bleu de Gascogne	17.0 (37.4)	Chesapeake Bay Retriever	29.25 (64.4)
Basset Fauve de Bretagne	12.5 (27.5)	Chihuahua, Longcoat	1.75 (3.9)
Basset Griffon Vendeen, Grand	19.0 (42)	Chihuahua, Smoothcoat	1.75 (3.9)
Basset Griffon Vendeen, Petite	13.5 (29.7)	Chinese Crested, Hairless	3.75 (8.3)
Basset Hound	21.0 (46.2)	Chinese Crested, Powderpuff	3.75 (8.3)
Bavarian Mountain Hound	30.0 (66)	Chow Chow	26.0 (57.2)
Beagle	12.75 (28)	Cirneco Dell'Etna	8.75 (19.3)
Bearded Collie	22.75 (50)	Clumber Spaniel	24.0 (53)
Beauceron	34.5 (75.9)	Cocker Spaniel	13.5 (30)
Bedlington Terrier	8.75 (19.3)	Collie, Rough	28.5 (62.7)
Belgian Shepherd Dog	28.25 (62.2)	Collie, Smooth	28.4 (62.5)
Bergamasco	32.0 (70.4)	Coton de Tulear	6.0 (13.2)
Bernese Mountain Dog	40.0 (88)	Curly Coated Retriever	34.25 (75.4)
Bichon Frise	–	Dachshund (L/H)	8.0 (17.6)
Bloodhound	43.0 (94.6)	Dachshund (Min L/H)	4.5 (10)
Bolognese	3.25 (7.15)	Dachshund (S/H)	8.0 (17.6)
Border Collie	21.25 (47)	Dachshund (Min S/H)	4.5 (10)
Border Terrier	6.0 (13.2)	Dachshund (W/H)	8.0 (17.6)
Borzoi	37.5 (82.5)	Dachshund (Min W/H)	4.5 (10)
Boston Terrier	11.5 (25.3)	Dalmatian	23.75 (52.3)

Breed	Average weight kg (lb)	Breed	Average weight kg (lb)
Dandie Dinmont Terrier	9.5 (21)	Japanese Chin	2.5 (5.5)
Deerhound	42.0 (92.4)	Japanese Shiba Inu	11.5 (25.3)
Dobermann	35.0 (77)	Japanese Spitz	6.0 (13.2)
Dogue de Bordeaux	41.0 (90.2)	Keeshond	27.5 (60.5)
Drense Partridge Dog	22.75 (50)	Kerry Blue Terrier	16.0 (35.2)
Elkhound	21.25 (46.8)	King Charles Spaniel	4.75 (10.5)
English Setter	27.75 (61)	Komondor	49.0 (107.8)
English Springer Spaniel	22.5 (49.5)	Kooikerhondje	10.0 (22)
English Toy Terrier	3.0 (6.6)	Lagotto Romagnola	–
Estrela Mountain Dog	40.0 (88)	Labrador Retriever	29.5 (65)
Field Spaniel	19.5 (43)	Lakeland Terrier	7.75 (17)
Finnish Lapphund	–	Lancashire Heeler	4.0 (8.8)
Finnish Spitz	12.5 (27.5)	Large Munsterlander	27.25 (60)
Flat Coated Retriever	29.5 (65)	Leonberger	52.25 (115)
Fox Terrier, Smooth	7.0 (15.4)	Lhasa Apso	–
Fox Terrier, Wire	7.0 (15.4)	Lowchen (Little Lion Dog)	3.0 (6.6)
Foxhound	30.0 (66)	Maltese	2.25 (5.0)
French Bulldog	11.75 (25.9)	Manchester Terrier	7.5 (16.5)
German Pinscher	–	Maremma Sheepdog	37.5 (82.5)
German Longhaired Pointer	26.25 (57.8)	Mastiff	83.0 (183)
German Shorthaired Pointer	26.25 (57.8)	Mexican Hairless	–
German Wirehaired Pointer	26.25 (57.8)	Miniature Pinscher	4.5 (10.0)
German Shepherd Dog		Neopolitan Mastiff	59.0 (130)
(Alsatian)	38.75 (165)	Newfoundland	61.0 (134)
German Spitz (Klein)	3.25 + (7.2 +)	Norfolk Terrier	5.25 (11.6)
German Spitz (Mittel)	11.5 (25.3)	Norwegian Buhund	15.0 (33)
Glen of Imaal Terrier	16.0 (35.2)	Norweigian Elkhound	20.0 (44)
Golden Retriever	30.75 (67.7)	Norwegian Lundehund	6.25 (13.8)
Gordon Setter	28.5 (62.7)	Norwich Terrier	5.75 (12.7)
Grand Bleu de Gascogne	33.75 (74.3)	Nova Scotia Duck Tolling	
Great Dane	50.0 (110)	Retriever	20.0 (44)
Greenland Dog	30.0 + (66 +)	Old English Sheepdog	30.0 + (66+)
Greyhound	29.5 (65)	Otterhound	43.25 (95.2)
Griffon Bruxellois	4.5 (10)	Papillon	2.25 (5.0)
Hamiltonstovare	25.0 (55)	Parson Russell Terrier	–
Havanese	–	Pekingese	4.25 (9.4)
Hovawart	35.25 (77.6)	Petit Basset Griffon Vendeen	13.75 (30.3)
Hungarian Kuvasz	42.0 (92.4)	Pharaoh Hound	–
Hungarian Puli	13.0 (28.6)	Pinscher	–
Hungarian Vizsla	25.25 (55.6)	Pointer	27.25 (60.0)
Hungarian Wirehaired Vizsla	25.25 (55.6)	Polish Lowland Sheepdog	18.25 (40.2)
Ibizan Hound	20.5 (45.1)	Pomeranian	2.25 (5.0)
Irish Red and White Setter	29.5 (65)	Poodle (Miniature)	–
Irish Setter	29.5 (65)	Poodle (Standard)	–
Irish Terrier	12.0 (26.4)	Poodle (Toy)	–
Irish Water Spaniel	25.25 (55.6)	Portuguese Warren Hound	–
Irish Wolfhound	50.75 (111.7)	Portuguese Water Dog	20.5 (45)
Italian Greyhound	3.0 (6.6)	Pug	7.0 (15.4)
Italian Spinone	34.75 (76.5)	Pyrenean Mountain Dog	48.75 (107)

Average Breed Weights (continued)			
Breed	**Average weight kg (lb)**	**Breed**	**Average weight kg (lb)**
Pyrenean Sheepdog	11.0 (24.2)	Sloughi	24.00 (53)
Rhodesian Ridgeback	34.0 (75)	Small Munsterlander	15.00 (33)
Rottweiler	45.5 (100)	Softcoated Wheaten Terrier	18.25 (40.2)
Russian Black Terrier	–	Spanish Water Dog	–
St. Bernard	70.5 + (155)	Staffordshire Bull Terrier	12.75 (28.1)
Saluki	–	Sussex Spaniel	17.0 (37.4)
Samoyed	20.5 (45)	Swedish Lapphund	–
Schipperke	8.0 (17.6)	Swedish Vallhund	10.25 (22.6)
Schnauzer	15.0 (33)	Swiss Laufhund (Jura)	17.75 (39)
Schnauzer, Giant	–	Tibetan Mastiff	82.00 (180)
Schnauzer, Miniature	6.5 (14.3)	Tibetan Spaniel	5.5 (12.1)
Scottish Terrier	9.25 (20.4)	Tibetan Terrier	9.25 (20.4)
Sealyham Terrier	8.5 (18.7)	Weimaraner	35.25 (77.6)
Segugio Italiano	23.25 (51.2)	Welsh Corgi (Cardigan)	10.75 (23.7)
Shar Pei	22.75 (50)	Welsh Corgi (Pembroke)	9.5 (21)
Shetland Sheepdog	–	Welsh Springer Spaniel	18.0 (40)
Shiba Inu	11.5 (25.3)	Welsh Terrier	9.25 (20.4)
Shih Tzu	6.25 (13.8)	West Highland White Terrier	8.5 (18.7)
Siberian Husky	21.5 (47.3)	Whippet	12.75 (28)
Skye Terrier	11.0 (24.2)	Yorkshire Terrier	2.75 (6.1)

described in advertisements as a 'deliberate cross, 10 weeks, excellent temperaments [*sic*], black and white and blue roans, wormed, jew [*sic*] claws removed, very long ears must be seen, both parents can be seen, £200'. *Caveat emptor*.

Many of these are advertised in free publications, a source, for a puppy that is best avoided. unless you are prepared to provide a home for a Honeywell Spaniel x tricoloured, a long haired Jack Russell, a Labrador X GSD, or an English Bull Mastiff x bitch.

Vulnerable Breeds

We Englishmen are marveilous gredy gaping cormorants of things that be seldome, rare, strange and hard to get.

William Topsell, *Historie of the Foure-Footed Beastes* (1607)

The passage of time has not eroded the truth of William Harrison's claim made in 1577 in his Description of England, in which he said that, 'There is no countrie that maie (as I take it) compare with ours in number, excellence, and diversitie of dogs.' Unless existing preferences have virtually already made the decision, perhaps some new owners might consider the attractions and qualities of one of the neglected native breeds. Some of these historically significant breeds hover on the edge of extinction to an extent that has given rise to Kennel Club concern: Bloodhounds, Deerhounds, Otterhounds, Irish Red and White Setters, Curly Coated Retrievers, Clumber Spaniels, Field Spaniels, Irish Water Spaniels, Sussex Spaniels, Dandie Dinmont Terriers, Smooth Fox Terriers, Glen of Imaal Terriers, Manchester Terriers, Kerry Blue Terriers, Norwich Terriers, Sealyham Terriers, Skye Terriers, Welsh

Terriers, Cardigan Welsh Corgis, English Toy Terriers, King Charles Spaniels all fail to reach the 250 registrations that might be regarded as a minimum if the breeds are to become less vulnerable. Some breeds retain a tenuous grasp on their existence with fifty or fewer registrations, while the most popular breeds record over 35,000. At the moment, concern is being expressed about the future of the orang-utan, about 25,000 of which exist in the wild and a significant number in captivity. A dog breed that has fewer than 2,500 registrations a year would have a population smaller than that of the orang-utan.

During the war of 1939–45 a number of breeds were brought to the verge of extinction. Some were saved after the war by importing stock from countries that had been less affected by hostilities, but the position of several remained precarious. The absence of concerted efforts to restore them to the former popularity that they undoubtedly deserved meant that they remained on the verge of disappearing. Efforts were made to draw attention to their plight, but it was not until 2003 that the Kennel Club embarked on a strategy intended first to assess the problem and then to tackle it.

That an appropriate strategy could achieve success had been demonstrated by the Rare Breeds Survival Trust that had devoted its attention to farm stock that had been overtaken by more commercial breeds but which carried a reservoir of genes that, in the future, might be needed to produce disease-resistant stock, to improve fertility or which were capable of thriving in other than intensive husbandry regimes. Much the same process was taking place to save plants carry genes that might be of use in the future.

It cannot really be argued that the genes carried by vulnerable breeds of dog would have any use but to provide material to improve the health of other breeds, or simply in order to perpetuate an important part of Britain's heritage, much as we preserve old buildings, works of art or artefacts whose practical use has long since disappeared. Even without economic justification the exercise is worthwhile in order to perpetuate variety, a part of Britain's heritage and to create interest.

Cosmetic Surgery

Our own species is pathologically wedded to the belief that appearance can be enhanced by means of surgical intervention, either trivial or more radical in nature. The industry is a lucrative one, and what we practice on ourselves is likely to be practised on others. For instance, the surgical removal of part of a dog's ears, cropping or in a less severe form rounding, is still practised in many countries. In Britain it became illegal at the turn of the end of the nineteenth century.

Docking

It is necessary for several reasons to cut off the tip of a Spaniel's stern when it is a whelp. First, by doing so worms are prevented from breeding there; in the next place, if it be not cut he will be the less forward in pressing hastily into the covert after his game; besides this benefit, the dog appears more beautiful.

Nicholas Cox, *Gentleman's Recreation* (1674)

Docking, the surgical removal of part or the whole of an animal's tail undoubtedly, has a cosmetic effect, but is seldom justified solely because of this. It was used by Alcibiades to disfigure and reduce the ability of a hound. For hundreds of years it was regarded as a prophylactic against rabies. It has been used as a means to identify certain types of dog

Puppies appeal across the generations.

per cent. Thus docking prevented tail injuries in about one in a thousand urban dogs. Mongrels are sometimes docked, but the justification can only be based on cosmetic considerations.

In most cases the operation is a trivial one that gives rise to no more than momentary discomfort. Done by inexperienced people, on puppies more than a few days old or by taking virtually all the tail it can be traumatic. Having persuaded the government to outlaw docking by laymen, the veterinary profession appear to have relegated it in their order of priorities. When breeders docked their own puppies the veterinary profession derived no income from the operation, but now that only they are allowed to dock all the income goes into their pockets. Economics appears to have modified what were once paraded as strongly held principles. Vets continue to practise docking as well as condoning other forms of non-therapeutic surgery in several other species and to justify it on economic grounds or as a means to avoid the consequences of standards of husbandry that a growing number of people regard as abhorrent. The debate will become academic if Parliament fulfils its declared intention to make docking for cosmetic reasons unlawful.

Prospective owners who regard docking as offensive should select an undocked breed or an undocked individual from a traditionally docked breed. If the intention is to become involved in some activity in which particular breeds excel, it would not make sense to select a breed that lacks ability in that particular activity.

and has been claimed as a necessary means to prevent tail injuries in working dogs or to prevent guard dogs from being incapacitated. It is sometimes justified as a means to improve hygiene.

As a prophylactic practice to avoid tail damage in working dogs the arguments for or against are complex and may vary from breed to breed. As a means to prevent tail damage in urban dogs the available evidence does not justify the practice. A study by P.G. Darke and others ('Association between tail injuries and docking in dogs', *Vet. Rec.*, 13 April 1985) showed that about 0.4 per cent of undocked dogs suffered tail damage, whereas in undocked dogs the figure was 0.3

Coat Type

All breeds require and deserve regular grooming but some carry profuse coats that need constant and often expert care. Owners who do not relish the prospect of grooming their dog on a daily basis or of incurring the cost of professional grooming should, perhaps, consider a breed whose coat is somewhat less demanding of constant attention.

Exercise

All breeds need some form of exercise and opportunities to explore and to play, preferably with other dogs, but toy breeds are less demanding in this respect than the sporting breeds. An owner who is unable, for whatever reason, to give a dog extensive exercise should take this into account when choosing a breed. Brachycephalic breeds should not be exercised during the heat of the day.

Sex

The pros and cons of neutering will be considered elsewhere, but, assuming that an owner intends not to subject his dog to emasculation, a number of points arise. The old adage that 'bitches are in season twice a year, but dogs are in season every damned day' contains a nugget of truth. Dogs may roam in order to find bitches in season. Bitches will roam only to find a mate when they are in season, though both sexes may also roam for other reasons. A bitch in season may become intolerant of other bitches or may she encounter hostility from formerly friendly kennel mates.

The choice – dog or bitch – may be based simply on personal preference, but attempts have been made to rationalize the choice in a survey of the behavioural characteristics of pure-bred dogs in the United Kingdom, (J.W.S. Bradshaw, D. Goodwin, A.M. Lea and S.L. Whitehead, 'A survey of the behavioural characteristics of pure-bred dogs in the United Kingdom', *Vet. Rec.*, 11 May 1996.) The survey covered only about one-third of recognized breeds and so provides only limited guidance as to breed characteristics. Females tended to rate higher than males for obedience training, ease of house training and were more demanding of affection. Males tended to be more playful, more active, more destructive, snapped more often at children, were more excitable, barked more, were better watchdogs, were more inclined to defend territory, were more aggressive towards other dogs and to dominate their owners. The survey accepted that both genetic variation and the early social environment played important roles in the development of behaviour but did not quantify them. It is, however, reasonable to assume that puppies that have not been carefully socialized in a home setting are most likely to grow into adults whose undesirable characteristics may be heightened. The wisdom of buying from a reputable breeder is thus further underscored.

The survey did not mention, let alone investigate, the role played by confidence. However, every scrap of empirical evidence that exists suggests that puppies born to confident parents, that are regularly and kindly handled from birth, that have been subjected to a variety of external stimuli, have played with toys, with one another, with adults dogs and with their breeder, are far more likely to grow into well-adjusted adults than are puppies that have been reared without benefit of these experiences.

Physique

Even the relatively small number of breeds recognized by the Kennel Club include a huge range of shapes and sizes. These include the brachycephalic breeds, with ultra short faces that may give rise to breathing and dental problems. Large, drooping ears are more inclined to harbour parasites and infections than small, erect ears. Long backs are more prone to spinal injury and

Dogs from different breeds and of different sizes may live amicably together.

which may include social aspirations, novelty, previous experience and recommendations from friends, but, in spite of what tabloid reporters may have their readers believe, seldom is choice influenced by the breed of the most recent Cruft's 'Best in Show' winner. Perhaps the most influential factor that drives up the popularity and cost of a particular breed, and sometimes to its detriment, is its use to promote some commercial product or association with television programmes or celebrities. Such breeds are best avoided until their popularity and cost begin to decline.

On-going costs include food and housing, both of which are obviously far higher for large, active breeds than for small, indolent ones. Veterinary fees as well as insurance will be greater for breeds with a history of ill health than for those which, given proper care, tend to remain in good health well into old age. Grooming too can be a continuing cost if someone acquires a profusely coated breed but does not want to undertake the daily grooming necessary.

Nevertheless, the cost of acquisition can represent a significant outlay. Buyers should beware – the most expensive puppy is not necessarily the best and the cheapest is not necessarily the worst. The worst puppy out of a litter bred by a good breeder may well be far better, especially when the effects of rearing and socialization are taken into account, than the best from a breeder whose prime motive is profit. Puppies should be bought from breeders who have a good reputation, and wise buyers are prepared to wait until a suitable puppy becomes available.

inherited dysfunction than shorter backs. Long-legged breeds tend to require a great deal of free exercise.

Cost

The cost of acquisition appears seldom to impinge heavily on the choice of breed. Still less are the costs of feeding and upkeep taken into account. The initial cost is not related to size but to indefinable criteria

Longevity

One factor that may influence the choice of breed is longevity. Dogs, when compared with people, have relatively short lives. They are expensive to acquire and may become

Dogs are adept at improvising toys and games.

expensive to care for in old age. Brachy-cephalic and giant breeds tend to have shorter lives than do medium-sized breeds that have no exaggerated physical features.

Temperament

A sociable and equable disposition should be regarded as a sine qua non for any dog. Much that is critical is said and written about the effect of dog shows, usually by people who have little experience of them and even less of breeding dogs. Show dogs are taken from their customary regime, transported to distant shows, introduced to unfamiliar surroundings and are expected to mix amicably with unfamiliar dogs and people. They will be subjected to a thorough and sometimes unceremonious examination by a judge and will be expected to accept all this with good humour. It would be difficult to devise a more demanding test of any dog's temperament than arises out of a career in the show ring.

There are good reasons for patronizing breeders whose puppies have done well in the show ring. Show dogs are bred to conform to detailed breed standards that set out the physical appearance and temperament of each breed. Konrad Lorenz fulminates against 'some of the nervous and vicious show specimens'. The breed standard of the breed against which he directs his principal ire lays down that the temperament should be 'steady of nerve, loyal, self-assured, courageous and tractable. Never nervous, over-aggressive or shy.' Lorenz's view contrasts sharply with the fact that nervous dogs seldom if ever achieve show ring success, and with the fact that any vicious dog would be barred from dog shows.

The breed standards of many breeds include a reference to temperament that breeders regard as very important: Bearded Collies are required to be 'steady, intelligent … with no signs of nervousness or aggression'; Bernese Mountain Dogs should be 'self-confident, good natured, friendly and fearless. Aggressiveness not to be tolerated'; Boxers 'equable, biddable, fearless, self-assured'; Dobermanns 'bold and alert. Shyness or viciousness very highly undesirable'; among Toy breeds Chihuahuas should be 'gay, spirited and intelligent, neither snappy nor withdrawn'; Pugs are 'even tempered, happy and [with a] lively disposition'; and Yorkshire Terriers 'spirited with even disposition'; in the Hound Group Basenjis are described as 'intelligent, independent, but affectionate and alert'; Basset Hounds 'placid, never aggressive or timid. Affectionate'; Irish Wolfhounds, one of the largest breeds in existence, have a 'gentle, kind and friendly nature'; among the popular gundog breeds English Setters are described as 'intensely friendly and good natured'; Irish Setters are 'demonstratively affectionate'; Labradors are 'intelligent, keen and biddable, with a strong will to please. Kindly nature, with no trace of aggression or undue shyness'; the Terrier breeds are sometimes regarded as snappy and pugnacious and this is sometimes excused by their former and current employment; Bull Terriers, in spite of their gladiatorial history, are 'of even temperament and amenable to discipline'; Cairn Terriers are 'fearless and [with a] gay disposition; assertive but not aggressive'. There is no need to go further, the point is made. Most pedigree breeds are required to have good temperaments that enable them to take their place in society as reliable and trustworthy companions.

Appearance

In his book *Man Meets Dog*, Konrad Lorenz – acclaimed at the father of modern ethology, a prolific author of both scientific and popular texts and a Nobel Prize winner – expressed the view that:

> Just as I am unable to think of any great intellectual who physically approaches anywhere near to an Adonis, or of a really beautiful woman who is even tolerably intelligent, in the same way I know of no 'champion' of any dog breed which I should ever wish to own myself.

The statement calls for no further discussion other than to point out that Konrad Lorenz was a very handsome man.

The offspring of successful show dogs can reasonably be expected to reflect the qualities of their parents. This may not be the case for the products of indiscriminate breeding. No one should underestimate the pride that derives from owning a good specimen of any breed.

Such considerations apart many new owners will often have a firm predilection for a particular breed for which they are prepared to make considerable sacrifices. In these cases choosing a breed is no more logical than choosing a spouse!

3 Benefits

In most urban environments dogs and cats are normally well integrated into the community as pet animals. ... They bring extensive benefits by providing companionship and protection to a large number of people.

World Health Organization (1981)

Men and Animals

In 1997 Stephen R. Kellert and Edward O. Wilson postulated in their *Biophilia Hypothesis* that humans have an innate need to learn about and have contact with species other than their own. The *Biophilia Hypothesis* argued that, without adequate interaction with nature, aesthetic, intellectual and spiritual needs remain unfulfilled and that children who are exposed to animals in a learning environment learn more quickly than those who are deprived of this association. Although the hypothesis was regarded as controversial in some quarters, the fact that man's relationship with dogs has existed for over 100,000 years cannot have done other than ingrain the need to continue the relationship.

Rather late in the day and far too late for some species, man is now beginning to realize that he has a responsibility to protect the future of other creatures with which he shares the planet. The lesson is driven home by such popular sages as Sir David Attenborough, Desmond Morris and Bill Oddie, and is marked by the popularity of books, television programmes and films about animals. It was only during the Industrial Revolution that people for the first time in history were becoming divorced from their agricultural roots to gather in the rapidly growing conurbations in which the scope to keep pets was limited. Even so, pet keeping burgeoned during this period and this provided the impetus that gave rise to competitions in which dogs and their owners could become involved.

A seminar of the Federation of European Companion Animal Veterinary Surgeons (FECAVA), held in late 2003, highlighted some of the advantages of pet ownership as well as some of the negative aspects. The seminar discussed the way in which attitudes to pet ownership had changed over the millennia and that the importance of a social interaction between people and some species other than their own was increasingly regarded as making a beneficial contribution to the quality of life. Dr Dennis Turner, president of the International Association of Human–Animal Interaction Organizations (IAHIO), stressed that in recent years pet ownership was playing an increasingly important role, with about half of all western households now owning at least one pet. Studies had shown that there were numerous benefits that accrue from pet ownership: social contact between people was promoted

Hunting is not the prerogative of the upper classes as some politicians seem to believe.

whether on an informal basis between people who share an interest in a particular pet species or more formally in children's and old people' homes, hospitals and prisons and other institutions in which people may be confined. Pet owners reported fewer ailments than non-owners and survived longer after heart attacks. The US National Institutes of Health had proposed that future studies of human health should consider the presence or absence of a pet in the home as one of the variables that impinge on health. Turner stressed that persuasive evidence was available that supported the thesis that pet ownership was associated with improved mental and emotional well-being. It had been shown to have a beneficial effect on pet owners' quality of life.

The Alternative View

Dr Tiny de Keuster addressed the negative aspects of pet ownership, largely concentrating his attention on dog ownership. He drew attention to the fact that surveys carried out in Belgian hospitals revealed that 94 per cent of incidents in which a child was bitten occurred in the home. Of the bites that occurred outside the home only 2 per cent involved dogs on a leash and half involved unaccompanied dogs running loose. De Keuster set these statistics in context by pointing out that dog bites were responsible for 0.23 per cent of all children seen in emergency departments During the same period four times as many children were involved in road traffic accidents and three times as many were treated for burns sustained in the home.

It is interesting and salutary to compare the seminar's conclusions with the evidence collected following the British government's iniquitous Dangerous Dogs Act 1991, based on little more than a politically inspired knee jerk reaction to a few tabloid headlines that disproved the adage that, when dog bites man it is not news, but when man bites dog that is news. Following the Act's

Children and dogs make ideal companions for one another.

implementation, a survey was carried out in the Aberdeen Royal Infirmary Accident and Emergency Department (B. Klaassen and others, 'Does the Dangerous Dogs Act protect against animal attacks: a prospective study of mammalian bites in the Accident and Emergency department', *International Journal of the Care of the Injured*, vol. 27, no. 2, 1996). The study was limited both in time and extent and by being carried out in only one A & E unit, even so, it did produce worthwhile data. It demonstrated that 73.9 per cent of all bites were inflicted by dogs, but also showed that human bites accounted for 17.9 per cent; bites by cats accounted for 7.5 per cent of the total. In terms of biting incidents, German Shepherd Dogs (Alsatians) with 24.2 per cent of all cases and mongrels with 18.2 per cent were the most inclined to inflict bites. The breeds whose alleged behaviour gave rise to the Dangerous Dogs Act – Pit Bull Terriers, Rottweilers and Dobermanns – together produced 6.1 per cent of all reported bites. They were less dangerous than either cats or people. Unfortunately, the survey did not relate the number of bites to the total population of the breed; if population had been taken into account German Shepherd Dogs and mongrels would have been relegated well below some less popular breeds. However, as a measure of the effect of the Act, the survey conclusively showed that in reducing the incidence of bites it had had no discernible effect.

Uses

It seems likely that dogs and people first developed a joint hunting strategy that would enable hunting expeditions to be more successful and to involve quarry that might have been too strong or too big for either partner to tackle alone. As wolves lost their fear of man, they would have lived closer to his dwellings, helping themselves to discarded scraps of food, providing man with warning of and protection from predators. As time passed, dogs, as they had become, were used for fishing, hauling loads, finding miscreants and testing the wholesomeness of food and were, as turnspits, even involved in the cooking process. When man began to create his gods, dogs were sometimes pressed into service in that role or as attendants of the gods. At other times they were punished for being the familiars of witches. During the last few thousand years the roles that dogs have been expected to play have increased, though all are based on the qualities that gave rise to the original association between dogs and man. Dogs have even been pressed into service as space travellers and they continue to benefit society in general as well as individuals. Archaeological remains demonstrate the dogs have been an integral part of British society at least since Neolithic times dogs have been an integral part of British society. The different types of dog produced by our ancestors demonstrate that they were talented breeders who used dogs for a variety of purposes. At least since the Roman occupation their talents have been recognized and British bred dogs have been and still are exported to almost every part of the world.

Economic Aspects

Some years ago the RSPCA commissioned the London School of Economics to carry out a report intent on revealing the cost to the country of keeping dogs as pets. The exercise was an unfortunately one-sided one, which could have done nothing to protect animals from cruelty but which, in some circumstances, might have engendered an attitude that may have exposed them to cruelty. It discussed the debit side of the account but totally ignored to focus on any of the benefits, social or economic, that flowed from dog ownership in Britain. The LSE's analysis ran counter to others carried out in other parts of the world that were perhaps of a more robustly independent nature. Surveys carried out in 1995 and 1996 in Australia and Germany showed that the benefits of cat and dog ownership on people's health saved $2.2 billion and DM 9.2 billion. If the same pattern was repeated in Britain, the saving to the National Health Service would be in the order of £1 billion, about half of which could be attributed to dog ownership. If companion animals were given to elderly people their health would be improved and their lives lengthened (but this would mean that they drew their pensions for a longer period of time which providers might not welcome).

An interest in dogs also sustains a wide range of industrial enterprises. The turnover of the pet food industry and of the pharmaceutical industry, even without the substantial contribution made by publishers, equipment manufacturers, grooming parlours, trainers, boarding kennels and other related enterprises, has to be measured in billions of pounds. Almost three-quarters of veterinary turnover derives from companion animals, without which the profession would virtually disappear, with a consequent disastrous effect on the ability to provide an adequate service to sick animals of all species.

Children empathize with most breeds.

Social Gains

The perceived benefits of dog ownership are almost as tangible as those that can be measured. Elderly people in particular have listed what they regard as the benefits that derive from pet ownership (Dorothy Walster 'Why not prescribe a pet?', *Geriatric Medicine*, April 1982). At the top of their list was the fact that a pet gave them something to do and something to talk about, with an interest in its behaviour, something to talk to and as a way of establishing contact with other owners also being regarded as important. Some older people living alone may become apathetic about their own welfare but will ensure that a pet has good living conditions and so themselves derive benefit from the association. A pet may also help them to cope with the death of friends, although they will also grieve as much at a pet's loss as they would that of a friend. Even confusion that is often the attendant of old age may be reduced by the demands of a pet for food or exercise. Florence Nightingale wrote in *Notes on Nursing* in 1859, 'A small pet is

There is some evidence that suggests that dogs can anticipate the return of their owners.

often an excellent companion for the sick, for long chronic cases especially.'

Even without taking part in organized dog-related activities, owners, especially those with attractive or unusual breeds, find often find that they are approached by strangers who are attracted by the dog. They develop a circle of acquaintances, some of whom will become friends when exercising their dogs. Through the dog they may develop social contacts and friendships that did not previously exist.

Assistance Dogs

It might be stretching the point too far to describe sporting breeds or breeds originally used to herd or guard domestic livestock as 'assistance' dogs. The term tends, especially nowadays, to have a far more restricted use; that is not to say that dogs have assisted their owners in many ways for a very long time. Some breeds were originally used to retrieve fishing nets; some were used to 'bear away fleas' or to provide sick owners with warmth and comfort. In Tibet they were used to dispose of corpses. They have been regarded as talismans. They have even been used as tax collectors' assistants. For many years dogs have been trained to carry shopping baskets and to deliver newspapers within the home. In more recent years suitably biddable and intelligent ones have been used to assist physically impaired people. Dogs can even load and empty washing machines, activate alarms and perform many other tasks.

Guide Dogs

The picture of a dog that appears to be guiding a blind person appears on a house wall in Pompeii and so dates from some time before AD79. During the eighteenth century illustrations produced in England make it apparent that the use of guide dogs was not confined to a few isolated examples. The present Guide Dogs for the Blind Association dates, notwithstanding changes of name, from 1931.

Hearing Dogs for the Deaf

Carefully selected and specially trained dogs are supplied to profoundly deaf people in order that they can respond to sounds – door bells, telephone, fire alarms, etc. – that their owners cannot hear. They provide not only an important service, but also companionship for people whose disability tends to isolate them from society.

Pat Dogs

Pat dogs are privately owned dogs that pay

visits to hospitals, care homes and other institutions in which people are deprived of the many benefits that derive from contact with dogs. The dogs are outgoing, affectionate and well trained, and both they and their owners are carefully vetted. Contact through the Pro Dogs National Charity.

Search and Rescue

In 2003 a dog's ability to search and rescue was officially recognized by the Insch Golf Club which gave it honorary membership for the work it had done to find and retrieve many thousands of lost golf balls. More importantly, dogs are used to find people lost in hostile terrain, perhaps buried under snow or collapsed buildings. The use of dogs to find the buried victims of earthquakes and other natural disasters or under buildings destroyed by explosives has been well documented.

Seizure Dogs

The use of dogs to predict the onset of epileptic seizures in their owners has only recently begun to be explored. Dogs whose behaviour gives warning that a seizure is imminent can help their owner to avoid it or to reach a place of safety while it takes place.

Sniffer Dogs

The ability of dogs to recognize a variety of scents is increasingly being used by law enforcement and security agencies. Dogs are used to find hidden drugs, explosives, contraband money, toxic residues, guns and illegal meat, for example.

Therapy Dogs

During the nineteenth century in Gheel, in Belgium, handicapped people cared for animals in the hope that the contact would 're-establish the harmony of soul and body'. In the 1790s the York Retreat encouraged patients to care for animals and to treat them kindly. The Bielefeld Home for Epileptics in Germany kept dogs, horses and birds as a means to provide patients with diversionary interests. It is now generally accepted that contact with dogs can help people who are withdrawn and uncommunicative to make better contact with their fellows.

4 Responsible Ownership

Although dog ownership provides a large number of benefits to both owners and society at large, these are accompanied by a number of unavoidable responsibilities both to dogs themselves and to society.

A puppy using garden plants for shade and privacy.

There is no need here to embark on a philosophical discussion about whether dogs and other non-human species have rights. It is enough to insist that we, the most dominant and most destructive species on earth, have a responsibility to other species and in particular to the species that we take into our homes as companions. Nowhere have these responsibilities been better defined than in the 'five freedoms'. At the BVA Congress in 1999 Lord Soulsby constructed his paper around the five freedoms that Professor John Webster had defined and which Professor Colin Spedding, while he was chairman of the Farm Animal Welfare Council, had promulgated in 1993. The five freedoms referred to the conditions that every animal had a right to enjoy, but Lord Soulsby applied them only to companion animals. Both Spedding and Soulsby were careful to avoid referring to the contentious area of 'rights'. The five freedoms to which they each referred were: freedom from hunger; freedom from discomfort; freedom from pain, injury or disease; freedom to express normal behaviour; and freedom from fear and distress.

No one who could be regarded as humane could possibly argue against the proposition that every companion animal should enjoy each of these basic freedoms. Yet thousands of companion animals, including rabbits and other rodents and several species of bird, may spend their entire lives in solitary confinement in small and often dank cages. Each and every day of their lives they endure discomfort, distress and have no opportunity to express normal behaviour. Their owners are seldom prosecuted as a consequence of their careless cruelty.

Freedom from Hunger

The cost of feeding a dog over what, with good fortune, may extend to fifteen years or even longer is perhaps the greatest of the costs associated with dog ownership. The larger the dog, the more vigorously it is exercised and, if it lives in a kennel rather than enjoying the same degree of luxury as do its owners, the more nutritious food it will require. In puppyhood and in old age it will need a specialist food than may be appreciably more expensive than a normal diet. It might also be added that stuffing a dog like a Strasbourg goose so that it becomes obese is a freedom from which dogs should be protected.

Freedom from Discomfort

All dogs deserve to be provided with shelter that provides them with protection against heat, cold and damp. They need too to be able to excrete without soiling their beds.

Freedom from Pain, Injury or Disease

All owners should treat their dogs with kindness and should provide or seek appropriate, professional, remedial attention should the animals fall sick or be injured. Injuries may, however, occur as a result of unforeseeable accidents or in the course of sporting activity. Much the same may be said of human athletes and, while it might be argued that they face the risks involved in their chosen activity as a matter of choice, it cannot be argued that dogs can assess the possible risk of injury to them.

Freedom to Express Normal Behaviour

Dogs are not by nature solitary animals; their ancestors lived in small, strongly hierarchical groups. Domestic dogs still need to have contact with others of their kind and to acknowledge a pack leader, usually their owner. A solitary dog cannot express normal behaviour. It is a moot point as to whether a dog subjected to surgery to make it infertile can express normal behaviour. Some people, whose views deserve to be considered, also suggest that abnormal physical characteristics such as brachycephaly, devoicing, earcropping and tail docking to some extent deprive a dog of the ability to behave normally.

Freedom from Fear and Distress

It is surely not necessary to argue that their owners and anyone else with whom dogs may come into contact should not treat them in such a way as to give rise to fear or distress.

Breed Health and Welfare

In recent years, the work of the Kennel Club to safeguard breed health and welfare has accelerated. In part, this is a response to the threat of European legislation that could adversely affect some of our long established breeds and also part of the on-going desire to encourage the breeding of healthy dogs and to promote participation in canine activities.

As a means of achieving these aims, the Kennel Club has looked to its own publications to see how it can convey the message direct to everyone involved in the activities over which it exercises authority. First, there has been a universal addition to the Breed Standards, so that the faults clause draws attention to the breeding of healthy dogs. This clause in every Breed Standard now reads: 'Any departure from the foregoing points should be considered a fault and the seriousness with which the fault should be regarded should be in exact proportion to its degree and its effect upon the health and welfare of the dog.' Secondly, the Kennel Club requires registered societies to print the following health statement in all judging books, to raise judges' awareness of the need to promote healthy specimens in the show ring: 'In assessing dogs, judges should penalise any features or exaggerations which they consider would be detrimental to the soundness, health and well being of the dog.' The Kennel Club continues to review its publications, not least the Breed Standards, and recent amendments to several standards have been considered in order to emphasize the need to breed healthy animals.

Aggression

It has been shown that aggressive behaviour in Cocker Spaniels is closely associated with the personality of their owners (A.L. Podberscek and J.A. Serpell, 'Aggressive behaviour in English Cocker Spaniels and the personality of their owners', *Vet. Rec.*, 1997).

Knowingly allowing a dog that is known to be aggressive or is suspected of harbouring aggressive tendencies the freedom to indulge in its predisposition is an act of gross irresponsibility that is to be seen every day in parks and on many highways. If such a dog is not properly restrained and causes injury to another dog or animal or to a person the owner is liable for any damage that may be caused. The traditional belief that dogs should be allowed one bite has been replaced by one of zero tolerance. Dogs that show signs of savage disposition may be excluded or removed from activities authorized by the Kennel Club.

Hygiene

The lady who, when asked whether she regarded it as hygienic to have a bitch and her puppies in the kitchen, and replied, 'Oh yes, I always wash my hands before I touch them', was not wide of the mark. Hygiene is a two-way process that involves the owner taking steps to ensure that he or she does not transmit infection to a dog and doing the utmost to ensure that a dog does not transmit infection to its owner, to other members of the family or to livestock.

The simple solution to the problem lies in ensuring that dogs are clean and well groomed at all times and that, should they come into contact, whether directly or indirectly, with an animal likely to harbour infection, they should be thoroughly cleansed by grooming, by a vigorous rub with a towel or, as a last resort, by bathing, which most dogs dislike almost as much as do small boys.

No dog that is suffering from any transmittable infection should be exercised or taken to a place to which other dogs may have legitimate access. Nor should a dog that is not fully protected against infection be taken to places to which dogs that have not been protected have access. Such places are often accessible to cats, foxes, rodents, rabbits and other wild creatures that may carry and can transmit infections to domestic dogs as well as to people (*see* the section on zoonoses in Chapter 9).

Inbreeding

Breeders refer to matings between closely related individuals as 'inbreeding', to matings between less closely related individuals as 'line breeding', and to matings between unrelated individuals as 'out crossing'. Even for people well versed in a breed, a study of its pedigree will provide only a hazy idea about the extent of inbreeding it represents. For those with no detailed knowledge, all

Unsuitable toys are often more fun than safer ones.

they can hope to do is to use the pedigree to see whether the sire and the dam are closely or more distantly related. Matings between siblings, between parent and offspring and between first cousins should all give rise to concern for the health of the offspring.

Most breeds, certainly most of those of relatively modern origin, were formed by means of close inbreeding, the matings of closely related parents. Other breeds were inbred because they existed in isolated populations or because they did not exist in sufficient numbers to avoid some degree of inbreeding. It is debatable whether inbreeding created breeds or whether breeds, or as least distinctive types, encouraged inbreeding. Over time, breeders began to regard what had begun as a matter of necessity as a desirable way of breeding quality dogs. However, it has long been recognized that inbreeding reduces fertility, leads to the spread of inherited disease, reduces resistance to infection and produces delicate individuals. This view was based on empirically

derived knowledge, but had until recent years been little studied by scientists. There is now ample reliable evidence to be found that shows the effect of inbreeding; its malevolent influence is beyond dispute.

In the wild, taboos or social arrangements exist in most species that limit or avoid inbreeding. In addition, inbred individuals tend to be more susceptible to disease and to the effects of harsh conditions and so fewer of them would survive to breed than more robust individuals. In 1975 Lukas Keller, of the University of Zurich, embarked on a study of data from an isolated population of closely inbred song sparrows on Mandarte Island, Vancouver. He found that harsh winter weather killed all the members of the population who were the product of matings closer than between first cousins. Other studies revealed that similar effects were seen in other wild species, as well as in human populations that, as a result of religious taboos preventing marriage outside a particular sect or because of geographical isolation, became closely inbred. The effects of inbreeding were limited by the conditions in which wild species were obliged to live. In some respects these conditions also apply to domestic species. Veterinary skills have become increasingly sophisticated in recent years, reliable vaccines and worming compounds are now available, and standards of care are high, whereas formerly only the fittest and most robust survived long enough to breed. An effect is known as 'inbreeding depression', of which Bill Amos, of Cambridge University, has said that, 'Inbreeding depression decreases when a population expands, and increases if it shrinks.' The relevance to numerically small breeds, especially the vulnerable ones now being studied by the Kennel Club, is apparent.

Improvements in veterinary science and in pharmaceutical products have meant that the survival rate has increased dramatically. Puppies that would have died in infancy survived to breed and to pass their weaknesses on to another generation. The continuation of reliance by breeders on inbreeding as the means to produce dogs of high quality, but without the checks imposed by survival of the fittest, was facilitated by a combination of a reluctance to cull weak individuals, improved veterinary treatment, a wide range of effective pharmaceutical preparations and improved standards of nutrition.

The use of microsatellite technology now makes it possible to measure the degree of inbreeding in any individual, whether or not its pedigree is known. This facilitates more detailed work on potentially inbred populations and will help to ensure that homozygosity is maintained in captive populations of endangered species. Amos's work on this now makes it possible to identify the degree of inbreeding present in any breed. Karina Acevedo-Whitehouse, who is working with Amos, has studied sea lions in a California rehabilitation centre and found that sick

animals were inbred, whereas those that had been injured but had no disease were unrelated. Cancer was prevalent among the offspring of sibling matings.

This work suggests that the rehabilitating of sick animals may help to spread deleterious genes through the population and so produce more unhealthy young. The consequences of this are stark for conservationists who make such heroic efforts to restore sick animals to health. The implications are less stark when applied to dog breeding. Culling weak puppies is no longer the only option. It would be quite feasible to ensure that they were not used for breeding, and it may well be that, if the Kennel Club were to provide the means by which breeders could measure and publish the degree to which stud dogs and brood bitches were inbred, pedigree dogs might become far healthier.

Insurance

Insuring pet animals is far and away the fastest growing sector of the insurance industry. The reason is obvious. It is also the most profitable in that far more is taken in premiums than is paid out in claims. Insurers are also protected against the effect of catastrophic losses such as might occur in other sectors of the industry as a result of gales or floods. A study carried out in 2004 for *The Sunday Times* found that premiums for top-of-the-range policies were 500 per cent higher than a basic but adequate policy. Within two years the cost of premiums could easily have exceeded the cost of purchasing the dog. It certainly pays to shop around and to read the small print with great care.

Even so, insurance against third-party liability arising out of damage or injury caused by a dog is an essential part of responsible ownership. If a dog runs into the road and causes a traffic accident in which

Grooming can help to strengthen the bond between dog and owner.

people are severely injured or even killed, the dog's owner may face catastrophic costs.

A survey by MORI Financial Services has revealed that only one in six drivers bothers to protect his dog, himself and other road users by restraining dogs being carried in a car and some owners make no effort to protect their dog from injury. Lack of effective restraint may result in severe injury or death in an otherwise minor accident. It may not be long before insurance will not be available for dogs that are not properly restrained while being transported in a car or some other vehicle.

Another factor is that veterinary fees have risen significantly as treatment has become more sophisticated. Dogs that would, even a short time ago, have been euthanased may now be treated by specialists who hold out the hope of a cure of the condition. There may be room for some suspicion that vets are more willing to treat insured dogs than those that are not, and that veterinary fees may have risen as a direct consequence of the existence of insurance.

Owners who are giving consideration to insurance should read the associated conditions with great care; they should be satisfied that veterinary fees, including hospitalization charges and the full costs of referrals are covered and not excluded if further treatment for a particular condition becomes necessary. The full cost of care for a dog if its owner through illness or injury is unable to give it proper care should also be covered, along with the full cost of advertising and a reward if the dog is lost or stolen, and cover for the dog should continue while it is with someone other than its owner. Many policies will refund the purchase price, which may be much less than the dog's actual value if it is used for breeding or has achieved success in competitions. The dog may have been purchased for a modest price as a puppy but will have needed considerable investment in order for it to achieve success and a considerable monetary value that will inevitably decline as advancing age takes its toll. The policy should, therefore, cover the full replacement value of the dog and not merely its initial purchase price.

Security

Given that a dog is well fed the most important aspects of its welfare hinge around security. Security from wandering abroad and perhaps getting lost. Security from thieves. Security from the many and complex dangers to be found in the average household.

Dogs in Cars

Never leave dogs unattended in cars, whether ventilated or not, on days when the weather is even only slightly warm. The car's temperature can quickly rise to a point at which suffering to the dog and even death may be the result.

Waste Disposal

Disposing of waste matter by exercising a dog along a grass verge or in a public park nowadays exposes the owner to the risk of a substantial fine and never was a public spirited course of action. It was and is one of the reasons for political and public antipathy to dogs. Even so, all dogs create waste material that needs to be disposed of.

Several options are available; incineration is perhaps the best. Some people add the material to a compost bin that, if it reaches a sufficiently high temperature, should sterilize the material. Others bury it or make use of a buried container in which the material disintegrates and disappears. Neither practice kills all parasite eggs, larvae or adults, and so, unless burial is very deep, remain sources of future infection. A septic tank will deal with waste most effectively but it is an offence to discharge it into a public sewer or to include it in household waste.

Material that includes dressings from an injured dog or material from the birth of puppies is legally regarded as clinical waste for which there is a strictly enforced procedure but a very small amount of such material is easily burned. Of course, not all the waste is objectionable. Hair removed when a dog is being groomed is sometimes used to produce yarn and in the spring is welcomed by nesting birds.

Some local authorities are beginning to express concern that dogs' urine is killing trees and rotting concrete and metal lampposts. They have yet to publish any scientifically credible evidence to support these claims, but dog owners who are unfortunate enough as to live within the bailiwick of such an authority should take whatever steps may be necessary in order to avoid being accused of being instrumental in deforestation or the destruction of street furniture.

Diary

Keeping a diary of the significant events in a dog's life, when its permanent teeth erupted, when it came in season, when its coat was stripped, any first aid or veterinary treatment it may have needed, as well as more mundane matters, will build into a document that will enable the owner to predict certain events as well as to identify any departures from the norm. Not only are such documents of appreciable use but they are also interesting.

5 Acquisition

'That dog you sold me for showing, well, it's for sale.'
'Yes, it was when I had it.'

Anon.

Modes of Acquisition

The process of acquiring a dog is something that many people are ill-equipped to face. They may never previously have owned a dog and may have only a vague idea of how best to acquire one and of the responsibilities that are an inseparable part of being an owner.

There are four principal sources from which dogs may be obtained: they may be obtained from their breeder, who typically may produce no more than one or two litters each year; they may be obtained from puppy supermarkets who can offer a choice of many breeds, most of which have been obtained from puppy farms; or they may be obtained from welfare agencies, some of which provide services for all types of dog and others confine their attentions to a single breed; and there are dealers who may also be breeders.

No one would deliberately buy a dog that is not in good health and likely to remain so throughout a long life. Equally, no one would buy a dog that has a suspect temperament either by reason of being subject to ill-founded fears or which is inherently aggressive. Puppies are likely to encounter infections with which they cannot readily cope by being transported in large numbers, kennelled with puppies from other sources and fed on unfamiliar foods. Puppies produced in large numbers in big, commercial kennels are unlikely to have received the attention that is needed for them to grow into confident and friendly adults. Whereas a survey carried out in 1990 by the Consumers' Association, and supported by the British Small Animals Veterinary Association and the RSPCA, found that puppies bought from breeders or private individuals were far more likely to be in good health than those bought from dealers or pet shops.

Significantly, 74 per cent of puppies bought from the place in which they were born, whether from an established breeder or a private individual who bred puppies only occasionally, were described as being in good health, while 8 per cent were in poor or very poor health (2 per cent in the last group). The corresponding figures for dealers were 18 per cent in good health, 44 per cent in poor or very poor health (13 per cent in the last group). Pet shops were somewhat better, with 40 per cent of the puppies they sold in good health and 30 per cent in poor or very poor health (7 per cent in the last group). Rescue kennels, the other popular source of puppies, were little better than pet shops with only 36 per cent in good health and 26 per cent in poor or very poor health (7 per cent in the last group).

In 2000 Intervet published the results of a survey they had carried out among a large and representative number of breeders. It revealed that over 37 per cent produced only one litter during the year and almost 17 per cent produced none. Fewer than 1 per cent produced more than four litters. The figures were consistent with those for 1999. Over 98 per cent of breeders were actively involved in showing dogs, with over 11 per cent involved in agility, obedience or flyball competitions. Almost 46 per cent selected bitches primarily on the basis of temperament. Health was a major factor to almost 22 per cent and conformation to over 30 per cent of breeders in the survey. All but 3 per cent of puppies were reared either entirely or partly in the house, where they were exposed to a wide range of experience arising out of routine domestic activity; 90 per cent were played with every day and over 96 per cent were taken outside the breeder's home. Over 80 per cent of the breeders preferred their puppies to go to their new homes when or after they were eight weeks old. The majority preferred them to go to homes that had some previous experience of owning a dog. When they were interviewing prospective owners, the criteria that were regarded as of most importance were: being at home with the puppy, having a good knowledge of the breed, and being sensible people with a good attitude to the puppy,

The First Steps

Once the decision to become a dog owner has been made, it will be necessary to decide what sort of dog is to be acquired and then to identify a suitable source. In both cases the head should rule the heart, although it must be admitted that there may be nothing rational in the choice of breed. The choice between a pedigree breed, a crossbreed or a mongrel will, to some extent, be dependent upon whether the dog is intended purely as a companion, is intended to take part in some competitive, sporting, working or social activity, or be expected to deter male-factors. Several criteria must be carefully weighed.

No one should ever buy a puppy without first seeing its dam. Caring breeders would never dream of letting others find homes for their carefully bred and painstakingly reared puppies. Many even go so far as to inspect prospective homes, and the majority will question intending owners closely in order to ensure that the puppies are placed in the best possible homes. Most will also offer an excellent after-sales service and will make all their knowledge and experience readily available to new owners.

Nowhere does the adage that 'a good wine needs no bush' apply more strongly than among dog breeders. The best breed and rear puppies with care and perhaps only occasionally. Their reputation is such that they may have a waiting list of people wanting one of their puppies. If a dog is intended for showing, for obedience or to work in the field, to choose anything other than a dog whose parents have excelled at the same activity would be unwise. In effect, this means a pedigree dog from a successful kennel with a good reputation.

How does someone with little contact with dog people find a puppy of the chosen breed? The first enquiry might be to the Kennel Club, which runs a selective register of breeders with puppies currently available. The second approach might be to a breed club, whose secretary will be only too happy to provide a similar list. Go to one of the major shows, especially one of the breed's club events, and you will see a great many dogs and breeders who will be happy to help. Try asking the secretary of your local canine society or veterinary surgeon whether they can recommend a local breeder. The two

A painting by E. Hunt captures a well-grown litter.

weekly dog magazines also advertise puppies, but beware – never be tempted by advertisements in the general press, and especially if they mention several breeds.

If it is not essential that you buy a puppy, or if you would prefer to have an older dog, breeders occasionally have adults available. Perhaps they have ended their show or breeding career and have earned a place on someone's hearth, such dogs are usually available at prices far cheaper than a puppy. The breed welfare or rescue organization may also have adults available. Such a dog should have been thoroughly vetted by the breed rescue organization and so should be unlikely to have serious health or behavioural problems. The same organization should also be available to provide advice and support. Nevertheless, nowhere is the adage *caveat emptor* more applicable than when buying a used car, a horse or an adult dog. Sometimes dogs undoubtedly fall on hard times because of the straitened circumstances of their owners, but to take the view that none ever become available because of intransigent, unruly behaviour or ill health is to exhibit a touching and often misplaced regard for the honesty of one's fellows, whether they represent welfare agencies or act on their own behalf. It is both surprising and disappointing to learn that adult dogs acquired from one internationally known welfare agency were highly likely to be suffering from one or more of several health problems. The lesson is obvious: no matter from where you are considering acquiring an adult dog from be very careful indeed.

Some new owners give thought to the possibility that buying two puppies may have advantages over buying one: they will provide company for one another and so be less troublesome. Two puppies might avoid family jealousies that one might generate. They will get exercise by playing together. The idea is not without its advantages, but

neither is it without its drawbacks. Two puppies are harder to train than one, they get into at least twice as much mischief, create twice as much mess and are capable of being twice as noisy. Infections may be passed from one to the other and they will need twice as much grooming. Two puppies will age together and eventually the owner will have two elderly dogs and must face all the consequential problems. An alternative it to wait until the first puppy is well into adulthood before adding another one to the household.

Accredited Breeders

At Crufts 2004, the Kennel Club launched its 'Accredited Breeders Scheme'. The aim of this is to encourage the breeding of healthy, well-adjusted puppies, which in turn will provide potential puppy buyers with an assurance that the breeder has followed good breeding practices.

This initiative has been implemented to promote responsible breeders and in turn place puppies with better-informed owners, ensuring that man's best friend is given the best opportunity in life from the beginning. The Kennel Club hopes this innovative scheme will help promote the welfare of dogs by providing and developing a code of best practice to which all responsible breeders that register their dogs with the Kennel Club will aspire.

The Scheme sets out a list of requirements that breeders must follow in order to be recognised. These include: that breeders adhere to Kennel Club policy regarding the maximum age of breeding bitches and number of litters bred from them. That they make use of health-screening schemes relevant to their breed for all breeding stock. They permanently identify breeding stock by DNA profiling, microchip or tattoo. They socialize the puppies, as well as providing written advice on socialization, exercise, training and feeding and offer a 'post-sales' telephone advice service.

Kennel Club registrations continue to increase, and with 20,000 people already using the health schemes, the Kennel Club recognizes the importance of introducing this scheme. It is believed that it will go some way to assisting in the breeding and sale of healthy, well-adjusted puppies, providing them and their owners with the best possible start in life.

(Kindly provided by and reproduced with the permission of the Kennel Club)

Breeders who abide by the Kennel Club and Breed Club Codes of Ethics are forbidden from selling puppies to dealers. An analysis carried out in 2000 of litters recorded by the Kennel Club in 2000 showed that a total of 31,981 breeders recorded 49,070 litters containing 247,278 puppies. Only six breeders recorded forty or more litters during the year. The most prolific of these recorded fifty-nine, containing 204 bitch puppies and seventy-nine dog puppies, about 2.6 bitches to each dog, whereas overall the ratio was almost equally balanced between dogs and bitches. Bitch puppies tend to be in greater demand and command the higher prices. Breeders who produced just one litter during the year yielded more than half of all the puppies recorded. They would thus have time to devote to ensuring that these had the best possible start in life. Breeders who produced four or fewer litters during the year produced all but about 50,000 of the 250,000 or so puppies recorded. Breeding can therefore be regarded largely as a hobby activity and at worst as a cottage industry. A typical breeder (72.7 per cent of the total) owns up to three breeding bitches; only 13.9 per cent own more than four.

The Kennel Club maintains a puppy sales register that records breeders who have puppies available. The register is available only to breeders who produce four or fewer litters during a twelve-month period and thus avoids overtly commercial breeders.

Welfare Kennels

Dogs may find their way into welfare kennels for a variety of reasons. Those that have been micro-chipped should quickly be reunited with their owners. Owners who do not take this elementary precaution in order to protect the welfare of their dog may have neglected it in other ways. The dog may have been abandoned, and both before and after it was discarded may have become severely traumatized. Such dogs require much knowledgeable attention, patience and understanding if their mental well-being is ever to be restored. Not all welfare kennels are aware of what their inmates have endured before they were rescued, and in the sometimes short period during which they have cared for them may not have become fully aware of any problems they may have or are developing. A dog that is perfectly happy in kennels may react very differently when it is in a home and among a family.

Dealers never, and rescue kennels seldom, provide aftercare and then, because they lack specialized knowledge of and commitment to a particular breed, do so only in general terms. Acquiring a dog, whether puppy or adult, from welfare and rescue kennels should be done only in the knowledge that some dogs may be discarded by previous owners because of some intractable behavioural peculiarity that may not have come to the knowledge of the rescue kennels. Previous ill-treatment may have left them scarred, wilful, and even potentially dangerous. A survey carried out in a national rescue kennel (D.L. Wells and P.G. Hepper, 'Prevalence of disease in dogs purchased from an animal rescue shelter', *Vet. Rec.*, 9 January

1999) revealed that more than half (53.7 per cent) had been ill within two weeks of their acquisition, which supports the findings of previous surveys. Symptoms often included coughing and/or diarrhoea, both of which may have indicated the presence of parvovirus or distemper and both of which are potentially fatal. When a newly acquired dog becomes ill its new owners are rightly upset and are often faced with considerable and unexpected costs.

Puppy Farmers

Although DEFRA has proposed that Welsh farmers should be given subsidies to encourage them to diversify their commercial activities into puppy farming, no one should, whether directly or indirectly, buy a puppy that has been produced as part of a farming enterprise. Rearing puppies demands very different attitudes and skills than are necessary for farm stock. Even though standards of accommodation, housing and feeding may be adequate, a busy farm will not have the time available to spend with a growing litter in order that the puppies will be well socialized.

Sadly, the standards of accommodation, housing and feeding and of overall care that puppy farms often achieve leave a great deal to be desired. Local authorities often turn a blind eye to these places and some are even prepared to license their activities. Even some local veterinary practices, to the shame of the profession as a whole, are prepared to give these enterprises their tacit and active support.

Most puppy farmers sell their animals direct to dealers to whose premises they are transported by the crateful, but some advertise their stock in local newspapers, often using a separate advertisement for each breed they produce. This enables them to present themselves to gullible buyers in the guise of other than a puppy farmer. Some even go to the extent of using several names and multiple addresses in order to disguise the extent of their activities.

Apart from the poor standards of care endured by breeding bitches and puppies in these farms, a buyer should also be aware of the possibility that pedigrees may be works of imaginative fiction, there will be no checks carried out in an effort to avoid inherited defects and bitches will be mated at every season while they remain fertile. What then happens to them is perhaps best left to the imagination.

Dealers

The largest dealers run supermarkets at which almost anything to do with dogs is available, even the dogs themselves. Puppies of several breeds and of no discernible one will be displayed in cages alongside kittens, rodents, cage birds and decorative fish – all displayed to tempt the unwary buyer. They are the modern equivalent of the late and unlamented pet shops. The puppies will have been born and reared on puppy farms, transported to the supermarket and caged together, without thought of how each might subsequently be matched to its alleged pedigree or registration documents. Some of these puppies will be incubating diseases acquired from puppies from other sources. The vendor will offer no worthwhile aftercare or advice, whether general or breed-specific. The buyer will be cast adrift with an expensively acquired, often sickly puppy that may soon need prolonged veterinary attention.

These puppies are the fortunate ones. Spare a thought for those that remain unsold when their puppy charm begins to fade, when their appetites reduce any prospect of a profitable sale and when they have outgrown the available accommodation. Some

Nora Howarth returns to a favourite theme.

will be killed, skinned and their remains consigned to an incinerator. There have been numerous instances in which magistrates have acted with undue leniency towards dealers caught transporting hundreds of puppies, including some that were sick or dying. A fine which represents much less than the sale price of a single puppy is totally inadequate as a deterrent to this callous trade. The only effective way of protecting dogs from the cruelty practised by puppy farmers and dealers is to buy elsewhere.

What to Buy

Deciding whether a mongrel or crossbred puppy is the best choice or whether some recognized pedigree or unrecognized breed is to be the choice may not be easy. Mongrel and crossbred puppies bring with them a measure of uncertainty about their adult size and appearance, their temperament and long-term health. To some degree the purchase of a mongrel puppy may be the product of impulse, of pity for the plight of a litter that were neither planned nor anticipated and may well have been discarded by their breeder. Such puppies are unlikely to have had the best start in life and may already be emotionally scarred by their early experiences. If, for example, they were discarded before they were weaned and needed to be reared by hand, they may have learned to demand food from people and to react with aggression when their demands were not immediately satisfied. The early experiences of hand-reared puppies may not provide the sort of basis that will enable them to grow into well-adjusted adults. This is not a good basis for buying a puppy.

If you are attracted to a crossbreed it is, of course, essential that you see both parents. Welfare kennels are by no means the least imaginative in describing puppies of whose parentage they know nothing as the product of a cross between two well-known breeds when in fact they have no idea what the parents were.

If the decision is made to buy a pedigree puppy ensure that it is registered with the Kennel Club, but, even if it is, do not be inveigled into buying a dog that does not conform in every respect with the standard for that breed. Unfortunately, the Kennel Club still accepts for registration puppies whose colour does not comply with the breed standard but does endorse the registration documents in order to warn prospective buyers. Do not be persuaded to buy what is described as a miniature version of a breed in which miniatures are not recognized. There is every chance that such puppies may, in fact, be crossbred or runts. It is also unwise to buy any puppy whose parents are likely to give rise to offspring that might be confused with any of the breeds proscribed by the Dangerous Dogs Act. The police and some local authority officials seem to have no compunction about attaching a label to perfectly well behaved and responsibly-owned family pets and to regard them as dangerous dogs to be taken from their owners, held in kennels and eventually put down.

From time to time, young dogs that have failed to reach the high standard required of guide dogs, hearing dogs and sniffer dogs become available. They often make excellent companions.

When to Buy

Puppies, particularly new puppies acquired by novice owners, should be bought only when the prospective owner has done all that is necessary to ensure that it will have a permanent home and good living conditions. There is inadvisable to buy a puppy through impulse or sentiment. Puppies demand and deserve a great deal of attention; they need time to settle into their new home and regime. They should not be acquired immediately before the new owner is due to go on holiday or the family is likely to become embroiled in seasonal festivities.

Only when a responsible seller is convinced that a new owner has sufficient experience and time to cater for the needs of a puppy which is less than eight weeks old will he part with a one of this age. Eight weeks to ten weeks is about the optimum time for puppies to go to their new homes. By this time they will be quite independent but will not yet have become so imprinted on their breeder or other dogs that they are unable to adjust quickly and easily to a new regime. A puppy that has been well socialized and exposed to a wide variety of the experiences, such as are likely to be encountered in a busy household, will transfer to a new home more easily than the one that lacks confidence and experience.

Inspecting the Pups

All new owners will and should want to

inspect puppies before they make a final decision to purchase. They should not, however, expect to be allowed to see puppies before they are fully weaned and independent of their dam. Responsible breeders will want to ensure that their puppies are, as far as is possible, protected from any infections that may be introduced by visitors. When the pups are six or seven weeks old they can be inspected, but even at this stage potential purchasers should not arrive in force with assorted children, their own or others who may simply have been brought along for the ride, or with hangers-on. To do so not only betrays a degree of insensitivity towards the breeder but also towards the puppies themselves and may result in a breeder's refusing to part with any puppy. If, as often happens, an expert, usually self-styled and sometimes with little actual expertise, is included in the party, the breeder should be warned because the last thing he will want is for another breeder to introduce infection into his premises.

On this first visit the prospective owner will want to ask many questions and should certainly do so. The breeder will want to be assured that the puppy is going to a good home too, and will minutely question the purchaser.

Seeing the Bitch

Purchasers are strongly and frequently advised to see the bitch before they buy a puppy. Even though it must be taken on trust that the bitch they are shown is, in fact, the mother of the pups, the advice is sound for a number of reasons. The purchaser will have some evidence that the puppies were bred and reared on the premises and that he is not dealing with a covert dealer. He will be able to assess the bitch's temperament and state of health, although it should not be expected that, after satisfying the demands

of her puppies, she would be looking at her best. She may also be concerned at the attention being devoted to her offspring by a group of strangers. Due allowance must be made.

By the time her pups are about eight weeks old her mammary glands will be returning to their normal state. If they remain pendulous it may well be that her pups are not yet fully weaned or that she has reared a relatively large number of them in the past.

Breeding Arrangements

Buying a well-bred, carefully reared and healthy puppy will involve an appreciable outlay. The temptation to spread the cost by becoming involved in a down payment and several subsequent payments will never arise if you are dealing with an honest and caring breeder. Some, however, may offer what are described as 'breeding terms' that involve an agreement by the purchaser to provide the breeder with stud services or, more likely, one or more puppies from subsequent litters. Such arrangements have a tendency to need resolution by being placed in the hands of solicitors, and with the inevitable result that the purchaser's actual outlay will be several times greater than had the puppy been bought outright in the first place. A classic example of how such arrangements can go wrong was seen at the end of 2003 when J.P. Magnier and John MacManus became involved in an acrimonious and costly legal dispute with Sir Alex Ferguson about breeding rights to the racehorse Rock of Gibraltar. When, after several months, the dispute was brought to a close, the only winners were the legal representatives employed to resolve the issue. It is disappointing that the Kennel Club not only recognizes but in its regulations appears almost to encourage such agreements. The Kennel Club recommends that triple forms obtained from the Club should be completed and copies sent to it and to the parties involved. Only if these conditions have been complied with would the Kennel Club act to resolve any future dispute, otherwise resolution would require the intervention of solicitors, few of whom understand the implications of such an agreement. The best advice is for purchasers to stay well away from any arrangement that does not give them full ownership of and full control over their puppy.

Discarded Animals

Owners, for a wide variety of reasons, may discard their dogs. Even owners who have given the matter of acquiring a dog a great deal of thought and lavished a high standard of care on a dog may find that their circumstances change: the family may split up, an enforced change of home may mean that a dog can no longer be kept, it may no longer be affordable or a family member may develop an allergy to it. Most of these discarded dogs will be placed in welfare kennels, national, local, general, and dedicated to a particular breed. In 2001 over 10,000 dogs were placed in welfare kennels and of these about 70 per cent were rehomed. Most of the rest were euthanased either because they were not suitable for rehoming or because they were unwanted; this subject is considered at greater length in Chapter 15.

Selecting a Puppy

Potential first-time dog owners are usually not well equipped to make an informed choice when selecting a puppy. Nor are they necessarily equipped to find someone with the expertise capable of providing reliable guidance. A good, caring breeder with a reputation to protect can be relied upon to give good advice, provided that due allowance is made for his or her pride and enthusiasm. None of which should discourage a potential owner from doing his utmost to equip himself to make a sensible decision.

Having established where pups of the chosen breed are available and when the breeder will be prepared to allow them to go to new homes, the next step is to take the first opportunity to see the puppies and, just as important, the conditions in which they are being reared. Some breeders will have a list of people, waiting with whatever patience they can muster until a puppy becomes available. Some breed only to satisfy a demand from individual customers and others try to ensure that they have a constant supply of puppies available for casual buyers to select from. Most breeders will allow potential buyers to see puppies before they are ready to go to their new homes. This enables buyers to see the mother, who is unlikely to be looking at her best and may not feel well disposed to strangers who interfere with her maternal arrangements. Due allowances must be made.

At this stage puppies will take an interest in visitors but should not be handled by them. Strange people may carry strange infections. If the puppies are active, playful, plump and clean, the breeder's assurance that they are in good health can usually be taken at face value. A cautious potential buyer may be assured that the males are entire and that none of the puppies have umbilical or inguinal hernias or have any inherited eye problems such as entropion and ectropion.

Some breeders will expect a deposit against the purchase price, others are less business-like in their attitude. They rely on a well-honed instinct developed over several years of experience and will sell puppies only to people whose attitude satisfies their instincts. It is natural and understandable for a breeder to take pride in a well-bred, well-reared litter, but any that make exaggerated claims, that a puppy is sure to become a champion should be treated with scepticism. First-time owners should not expect and should be very cautious about any breeder who is prepared to part with a puppy until it is eight or more weeks old. Some prefer to have their puppies vaccinated before they go to their new homes, others prefer that new owners have the puppies vaccinated, and, at the same time, have an independent, general health check carried out.

Before a buyer goes to collect his puppy he will have made all the necessary arrangements at home to provide it with food, somewhere to sleep, security, toys and all the other things it may need. The breeder will supply a Kennel Club registration document for the puppy, a pedigree and a diet sheet containing basic advice about how best to care for the puppy. It will be made clear that further advice will be available at the cost of a telephone call. This service is seldom available from dealers or welfare kennels.

The buyer should expect to pay the full, agreed price before taking the puppy home. Arrangements that involve the new owner in a deferred payment agreement or in providing the breeder with puppies from a bitch should be avoided. Unscrupulous vendors may rely on a new owner's desire to own a puppy and the speed at which a strong bond is established between owner and puppy to protect the dealers against subsequent recriminations arising out of the puppy's ill health or unsuitability for its intended purpose.

6 Equipment

Basic Equipment

The vast majority of dog owners are anxious to do their best to ensure that their dog receives a good standard of care. Commercial firms who suggest that a dog is somehow being deprived unless it is provided with some particular, often useless, item too often exploit this anxiety. If it pleases the owner to indulge his dog with such things, provided that they pose no threat to the dog's well-being, all well and good. Sadly, this cynical commercialism is in one form or another to be found throughout the industry, even more sadly some of the items are not only useless but may even be harmful.

In order to take care of grooming a washable brush and comb appropriate to the dog's coat are required. A pair of sharp scissors may be needed from time to time (*see* below for more on grooming).

Feeding and drinking bowls should be appropriate to the dog's appetite. Good quality stainless steel or earthenware are vastly preferable to plastic that is not easily sterilized, is easily damaged by an enthusiastic dog and to which some dogs may be allergic. Bowls with a wide base and narrower top are not easily upset and help to keep pendulous ears out of food or water. If the feeding bowls are of a size that will comfortably accommodate a normal meal, it is easier for an owner to regulate the amount of food in each meal. The use of stands to support feeding and water bowls above ground level is convenient for exceptionally tall dogs and is said to go some way towards avoiding

bloat. Food, apart from tinned food, should be stored in vermin-proof containers.

Simple first aid can be carried out with materials to be found in any well-equipped household, nothing special is needed except in unusual circumstances.

Beds

All dogs need a place to which they can retire and in which their privacy is respected. The bed should be big enough for the adult dog to lie down at full stretch, provide comfort for it and be as close to indestructible as possible or should be easily reparable. The bed should also be easily cleaned. Some puppies are inclined to chew their beds. Until they have foresworn the habit a stout cardboard box will serve as a perfectly adequate bed. A competent handyman easily makes wooden ones and there is a wide range of different sorts available from retail outlets.

Kennelled dogs benefit from an enclosed wooden or plastic bed that protects them from draughts; but for a housedog there is usually no need for an enclosed bed, although there are times when it could be an advantage to confine the dog to its bed. The choice is largely between wood, plastic and wire mesh. Wicker beds may look attractive when new but are tempting to chew, impossible to repair and difficult to clean. If the bed is of a size that can be carried in the car it will be far safer and easier to transport the dog. If the bed is too big or the car too small,

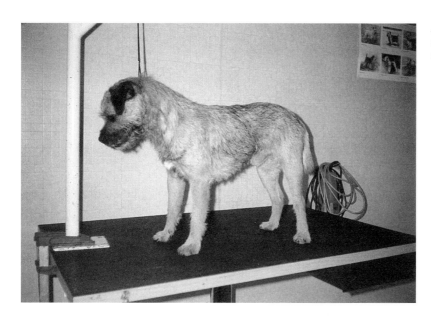

a collapsible cage might prove useful. A wide range of travelling crates and cages are available. Those that pose a complicated solution to what is essentially a simple problem should be avoided, as should those that are not easily cleaned.

Bedding

The type of bedding suitable for different breeds and in different circumstances varies almost endlessly. All bedding, however, should be capable of being easily replaced or thoroughly washed. Kennel dogs might be housed on sawdust, wood chippings, peat, shredded coconut fibre or on shredded paper, all of which have the advantage that they do not introduce parasites into the kennel. This cannot with certainty be said of straw or hay that may bring with them an unwanted population of fleas, ticks and mites. In addition, barley straw may bring sharp husks capable of becoming embedded in a dog's skin, where they may give rise to injury and infection.

For housedogs towelling is excellent, as is the faux fleece fabric now readily available in an assortment of colours. This is sometimes advertised as being indestructible – it is nothing of the sort, a determined dog is quite capable of reducing it to shreds in a short time.

Clothing

Although the macho image of the dog or its owner may be compromised, warm clothing will help to keep comfortable an old dog or one that is exercised sedately. Toy dogs and thin-coated dogs in particular will appreciate clothing.

Toys

A healthy dog will indulge in games either with another dog, its owner or, if all else fails, by itself until the desire is overtaken by advanced old age. Some people are inclined to be somewhat disdainful about this juvenile propensity, and then will invest time and energy in playing cards, chess or golf (a game that involves pursuing a ball). In fact, we have no reason to feel superior about our own choice of games.

Toys are often designed to be attractive to owners rather than to their dogs. A hard, nylon object is useful as a means to teach a dog to retrieve and to encourage it to take exercise. A hard rubber weight with a securely attached piece of rope serves the same purpose and is a plaything with which will keep a dog interested in playing with it. But there are few more mutually enjoyable and beneficial games than throwing a ball or a stick for a dog to retrieve – a ball small enough to be carried by the dog but not so small that it can be swallowed, or a strong stick that will test the dog's concept of balance and ability to negotiate narrow gaps. All toys and playthings should be chosen with safety as well as enjoyment in mind and particularly so if they are intended to be played with by an unsupervised dog.

Hide chews of unknown source should be avoided. Many are imported from Asia and may contain substances likely to be harmful. Flimsy plastic toys, even though they are sold in some veterinary surgeries, should also be avoided. Plastic shards may be swallowed and, being impossible to digest, may cause obstructions that require surgical intervention.

Kongs, which combine a heavy, almost indestructible bouncy weight with a short length of rope, are excellent toys either for retrieving or for a solitary game.

Leads

Leads come in all shapes and sizes. The traditional leather lead with a looped handhold at one end and a clip at the other remains a serviceable item of equipment, but rolled leather with an integral nylon reinforcement is less likely to snap when under stress.

Nylon strap, spring-loaded, retractable leads allow a dog a degree of freedom when fully extended and can be retracted to serve as a normal lead. For the show ring, a strong but lightweight slip with an integral collar is usually used. These do not detract from the line of the neck and can be quickly adjusted if necessary. At hunt and working terrier shows a length of binder twine is sometimes used as a means to give the impression, usually false, that the terrier has only recently been engaged in its regular sporting occupation. The impression is sometimes reinforced by the handler's chosen tweedy apparel.

Collars

The law currently insists that all dogs should wear a collar with a tag carrying the name of its owner and home address. It is difficult to imagine a better way of providing thieves with the information they need to take the dog, contact its owner and demand a ransom for its safe return. It has become even more asinine since it became possible to identify every dog with an implanted microchip.

The traditional way of curbing the enthusiasm of a dog inclined to pull when on the lead was to equip it with a harness. In fact, this simply enables a dog to pull harder without causing any discomfort to its neck. It might even be said to encourage a dog to pull, and, unless fitted with care, can make the dog sore around pressure points.

Only a simple, traditional collar and lead will be required, but, if a dog insists on pulling against a lead, a 'Halti', a modified head collar devised by Dr Roger Mugford, will usually solve the problem. When a dog pulls against this its efforts tend to turn its head away from the direction of travel, thus making progress more difficult, but when it stops pulling its freedom is regained. A retractile lead is also useful to give a dog a greater degree of freedom than it would have on a normal lead.

Some owners indulge their fancies by providing their dogs with ornamental, even jewelled collars. Others adorn their dogs and sometimes themselves with brass-studded collars. These provoke comments by some, but, provided that a collar fulfils its essential requirements, what harm is done if it pleases an owner to indulge in a little harmless ostentation? In any case, the fashion is by no means a new one: Leeds Castle in Kent houses a fine collection of dog collars, some hundreds of years old and very decorative.

Grooming

All breeds require regular inspection of their coats, ears, eyes, feet and teeth, some more than others depending on the breed and the conditions in which they live and are exercised. Regular grooming, every day for heavily coated breeds and every few days for smooth coated breeds, is an essential prerequisite to good health. The more frequently and thoroughly a dog is groomed, the more likely it is that developing conditions and the presence of parasites will be detected before they become serious threats to health or comfort, and the more likely then that they will respond to treatment by the owner and so not require veterinary attention.

Most dogs quickly become accustomed to the grooming routine and many show every sign of enjoying the experience, even if they do shake vigorously as soon as the process is complete. Grooming is not just a matter of brushing or combing the coat but should include a thorough inspection of the entire dog from teeth to tail.

Coat
Virtually every breed needs to be groomed in such a way as to preserve and enhance the appearance that first attracted the owner to it. People who know little about dogs may profess to be amused by what they claim to regard as needless hairdressing, yet they will not infrequently regard their own appearance somewhat differently.

Profusely coated dogs need skilful grooming if they are to conform to the appearance that may have attracted their owners to the breed in the first place – there seems little point in buying such animal and then trimming its coat to stubble. Not all grooming parlours are capable of providing the requisite level of skill, although the best certainly are. It is not within the scope of this book to provide information about how best each breed should be groomed.

Smooth-coated breeds need no more than a daily brush with a soft bristled brush, grooming glove or even a chamois leather.

Harsh-coated breeds, particularly those with a soft undercoat, need to be groomed with a somewhat stiffer brush or terrier pad and comb. Heavy growths of coat around parts of the body that are most likely to become soiled with mud, food or excrement should be carefully cut with a small pair of sharp scissors. Stripping knives that, in effect, are small-toothed, almost saw-like combs make it easier to remove dead coat but should not include a blade that will cut the coat rather than remove it. However, the best tool for stripping a dog remains the owner's finger and thumb. Proficiency takes practice to develop, but even a less than skilled attempt will do less harm than an unskilled use of grooming tools.

All but the smoothest of coats may occasionally become matted with either vegetable or some other matter that has become entwined in them, because the coat has been allowed to grow long but has not been sufficiently well groomed to prevent it from becoming matted. The best way to deal with mats is to remove them with a pair of sharp scissors.

Most breeds, Poodles and Bedlington Terriers being among the exceptions, shed dead coat in spring, but without regular grooming the process may be virtually continuous. Frequent and vigorous brushing can best reduce this.

Feet

Feet should be examined regularly to ensure that no foreign bodies or material has become attached to them. If a dog is exercised on roads on which salt and grit has been spread, its feet should be thoroughly examined and washed as soon as it reaches home or even, if an opportunity occurs, during exercise.

Nails

With the exception of the Norwegian Lundehund, which has an additional digit, all dogs, have four toes on the forefeet plus one or sometimes more dewclaws. They also have four toes, but only abnormally have dewclaws on the rear legs. Each digit is furnished with a nail, which, unless the dog is exercised on a hard, abrasive surface will need to be clipped from time to time. The dewclaws, which do not come into contact with the ground and are not subjected to much wear will need to be clipped more frequently. Some breeders routinely remove the dewclaws and the residual toe to which they are attached before the puppy has its eyes open, others leave the foot intact. The two schools of thought have not yet provoked the veterinary profession into taking a stand on one or other side. They may well avoid the issue because, if breeders were banned from removing dewclaws, they would simply leave them intact and no benefit would then accrue to vets.

A sharp pair of nail clippers is needed and should be used on a regular basis, depending on how quickly the nails grow, which is itself dependant on diet and exercise. If nails are regularly clipped, only the tip needs to be removed and the need to cut deeper and risk making the nail bleed and sore is avoided.

Teeth

Puppies are born without teeth. A set of milk teeth will erupt when the puppy is about a month old. These will consist in each jaw of six incisors, two canines and six premolars, making twenty-eight in all. The milk teeth are replaced by permanent teeth when the puppy is about seven months old. The completely furnished mouth consists of six incisors, four canines, four premolars and four molars.

Examination of the teeth should be an integral part of the grooming routine. The process should begin as soon as a puppy is installed in its new home and is likely to have already been begun by a breeder who is anxious to ensure that the formation of the jaw and the position of the milk teeth do not indicate that problems may occur when the permanent teeth erupt.

When examining a dog's mouth care should be taken not to obscure the dog's vision, something which the inexperienced and ham-fisted are often guilty of. This makes the dog inclined to try to escape from the examiner's grip and will make it reluctant to submit to the process in the future. The lips should be pushed back with the thumbs, while the fingers support the under jaw. This allows the incisors and canines to be examined. Examination of the molars requires one hand to be released in order to lift the lip covering the rear teeth. The examination should look for broken, badly worn and loose teeth, the presence of foreign material lodged between the teeth, swollen or bleeding gums and bad breath, which may indicate dental problems as well as digestive ones and even a worm infestation. Minor problems can often be solved by brushing the teeth and the use of a suitable canine toothpaste and by a change of diet.

If any milk teeth are retained after the permanent teeth begin to erupt and show no sign of becoming loosened by chewing suitable hard objects, they should be removed by a veterinary surgeon. Teeth broken at any stage during a dog's life also warrant veterinary attention.

A dog with a normal mouth and fed on a diet which includes some hard material, may well live a long life without the need for any professional dental attention. Advancing age may result in the teeth becoming dark, especially near the gums and to an accumulation of plaque which, although itself unharmful, may harbour harmful bacteria. Plaque is easily removed with a clean, blunt tool if the dog is prepared to co-operate.

Ears

There are no wild canids with large pendulous ears; they all have prick ears, sometimes sharply pointed, sometimes rounded and always mobile. Dogs with prick ears seldom need to have their ears cleaned, but the humid warmth in pendulous ears seems to provide conditions in which parasites and infection may thrive. In either case, a small amount of clean wax is normal and helps to maintain healthy conditions within the ear. Dirty or smelly ears are likely to be harbouring some form of infection that may, as it becomes more serious, cause pain and discomfort that will, in turn, cause the dog to scratch its ear and so cause yet further injury. A number of preparations exist to help to clean the ear and to eradicate parasites and mild infections. They should be used to clean those parts of the ear, including the earflaps, that are accessible to a finger. Using any instrument to probe further into the ear is likely to do more

harm than good. By keeping the outer ear clean and the hair under the flap trimmed and by frequent inspections for signs of infection, injury or the presence of foreign bodies the ears may be maintained in good health.

All dogs, but in particular those with pendulous ears, may injure their earflaps, either by pushing through dense undergrowth or in fights. The injury should be treated in the same way as injuries on other parts of the body, but if the dog is inclined to scratch at a dressing an Elizabethan collar will frustrate its efforts. These may be bought but are easily and more cheaply made out of a plastic container of an appropriate size.

Eyes

Some breeds have large, round and semi-protuberant eyes that are prone to injury, and all breeds during exercise might get foreign bodies into their eyes. This can be reduced by exercising those dogs whose eyes are prone to injury away from undergrowth or rank vegetation that might harbour material likely to become lodged in the eyes. Nor should any dog be allowed to travel in the car with its head out of the window: the dog may enjoy the experience, but there can be few ways more likely to cause injury or infection to the eyes.

Immediately after exercise the eyes should be examined for the presence of foreign bodies and these removed as quickly as possible before the dog's efforts to remove them itself make a slight problem into a potentially serious one.

Mouth

Apart from all the same uses to which we put our mouths, dogs, like human babies, also use their mouths to explore the texture of foreign objects and, as a consequence of any ill-judged exploration their mouths are subject to injury.

Runs

Runs may be either permanent construc-
tions, or, for small and medium-sized dogs,
large cages that provide some measure of
security. But the latter are usually not big
enough to provide space for adequate exercise; their big advantage is that they can be
moved in order to prevent the ground they
enclose from being fouled and to more or
less sheltered positions in the garden.

Bathing

Most dogs share with small boys a liking for
splashing about in water, but, again like
small boys, are not usually enthusiastic
about bathing. President Ford of the United
States solved the problem of bathing his dog
by encouraging it to share the shower with
him; this may be acceptable if the dog is
already clean but, if the dog has become
dirty or encrusted with objectionable material, to share its ablutions does not seem to
be a good idea.

Travelling Cages and Crates

In recent years a wide range of designs and
sizes of travelling crates have become available. Some seem to be unnecessarily complicated, others have very limited uses. A stout
wire mesh cage, either collapsible or not, is
ideal, and one preferably with a side opening
door that will allow the cage to double up as
a bed or place of retreat from unwanted
interference. Covers can be bought for most
cages and these provide both shade and protection from draughts. Plastic and stout can-
vas cages are equally good, but avoid wood
that is difficult to clean and invites chewing.

Gates

Self-closing gates provide protection against
thoughtless visitors who insist on leaving
gates open and seem oblivious to the possibility that dogs may take advantage of this to
explore. A simple notice reminding visitors
to close the gate securely is far better than
one that warns of the presence of a dog –
'Beware of the dog' not only informs thieves
of the presence of a dog but may also be
used in court to demonstrate that the owner
was aware of the possibility that the dog
might bite, if a visitor, going about his legitimate business, is bitten.

Gates with vertical bars sufficiently closely
spaced to prevent a dog from squeezing
through the gaps are better than horizontal
ones that an agile dog might climb. Better
still are solid gates that prevent the dog from
being seen or nosing at passers by.

7 Feeding

We find that Mr Smith, who introduced his biscuits on our Magazine cover, has met that encouragement and patronage which we trust will ever follow the endeavours of all who study to promote the pleasures and conveniences of the Sporting World. We have seen a letter from our valuable correspondent, NIMROD, who states: 'I approve of them very much, and shall not fail to recommend them to my sporting friends'; – also, from E. Cripps, Esq., whose black bitch, Emerald, won the Ashdown Cup, stating, 'I must say it is the best food for Greyhounds I have tried.'

The Sporting Magazine (1826)

Having spent over 100,000 years surviving on the scraps of food that man discarded, dogs have evolved so that they are able to survive and even thrive on a diet that would have been rejected by their wild ancestors. Dogs are by nature carnivores and so are adapted to eating their fill when food is available and going hungry when it is not. Owners who confuse a dog's pleas for food with actual hunger are likely to overfeed it with unfortunate consequences. Carnivores do not rely on meat as their sole source of nutrition. In the wild dogs eat other animals including the contents of their stomachs as well as fruit, grasses and other plant material. Domestic dogs still enjoy fruit and the tender shoots of some species of grass and their diet should reflect this.

Domesday book, which recorded the results of surveys begun in 1085, contained a reference to *ter mille panes canibus*, 3,000 cakes of dog bread, being produced in Chintenham (Cheltenham?), Gloucestershire. This reference taken with those in *Master of the Game* (by Edward, Duke of York, 1406) show that the manufacture of food intended for dogs was already established in the eleventh century. The industry is now a multinational one employing thousands of people and producing a wide range of products.

Commercial Dog Foods

Puppies grow at a far quicker rate than human babies. By the time they are about six months old they will have reached their adult weight, although larger breeds may not do so until they are about a year old. In order to sustain this rapid rate of growth they need to be fed at least three times a day on nutritious food. At this stage in their development they will be eating more than they will as mature adults. A breeder who cares about the future well-being of the pups he produces will have provided a new owner with a detailed diet sheet based on his own, often extensive, experience. Such guidance takes account of any particular peculiarities the breed may have: some breeds are intolerant of lactose, for example. Every container of commercially produced dog food will provide information about its ingredients for the purchaser. There are a great many proprietary foods formulated with puppies in mind, but not all may be suitable for every breed and thus the recommendations of discerning breeders are far more reliable than a manufacturer's advertising claims.

During the last twenty years the range of proprietary foods has been considerably increased. Tinned foods, consisting of about 80 per cent water, mixed with biscuits, now compete with semi-moist foods, with up to about 50 per cent water, and dry foods, usually with less than 10 per cent water. Typically, canned food has a kcal content per gram of about 0.75, semi-moist food of about 3.00 and dry food of about 3.5. Thus in order to produce the same energy level it would be necessary to feed an animal over four and a half times as much moist food as dry food. Even when moist food is supplemented with a good quality mixer, typically containing about the same energy content as dry food but far lower in essential nutritional elements, it would be necessary to feed about twice as much moist food and mixer as dry food.

In recent years, as the old prejudices of dog owners have been eroded, products improved and their range extended, the market share achieved by dry foods has grown dramatically. Once owners realized that tinned foods consist largely of water and dry foods of little other than nutritious ingredients, this is hardly surprising. The largest drawback associated with dry food is that it is essential that a supply of clean drinking water should be constantly available.

The range of products now available is bewildering, but the main difference between many consists of little more than their label and packaging. Once a satisfactory diet appropriate to a dog's age, size, living conditions and level of activity has been found it should be changed only as a matter of necessity.

Many owners indulge in a degree of anthropomorphism that leads them to vary their dog's diet and to give it extra treats at Christmas and other anniversaries. The result is that the dogs are likely to develop diarrhoea or even be poisoned. Any food given between meals should be a reward for good behaviour and not, as is often the case, what is in effect a reward for begging or pestering and which may only reinforce this unwanted behaviour. Titbits should be given sparingly and consist only of low calorie food; fruit and vegetables are ideal.

Not only do growing dogs require a more nutritious diet than do adults, but the same is also true of small dogs when compared with their larger brethren. For this reason some manufacturers have tailored products to reflect the dietary needs of dogs of different sizes. Similarly, working and sporting dogs or those that are called upon to endure hard exercise, those that do not enjoy the benefits of living in heated conditions, those in whelp and lactating bitches all need a diet that takes account of their increased nutritional needs. Older dogs may suffer from a number of age-related conditions that require special diets, such as nephritis or kidney failure; obesity diets, which are unnecessary unless the dog has been grossly overfed and under-exercised (*see* below), are also available, while convalescent dogs may require a diet that is more nutritious than its normal one.

Frequency

In their wild state dogs eat to repletion when food is available and go hungry when it is not. Domestic dogs are accustomed to a more regular regime, but, given the opportunity, may still eat to repletion. It is the owner's task to ensure that the amount of food is appropriate to their needs but not so much as to produce obesity, one of the greatest sources of ill health, or so little as to produce a weedy, half starved individual. Puppies should be fed three or four times a day, and convalescent, aged and nursing dogs (about which a more detailed exposition is to be found in *Dog Breeding: The Theory and Practice*, by Frank Jackson [The Crowood Press]), should also be fed more frequently than young animals. Breeds that may be prone to bloat should also be fed smaller and more frequent meals.

Whether a normal, healthy, adult dog should be fed once or twice a day is a matter for the owner's judgement and the routine that the dog normally enjoys. It is unkind to feed a house-trained dog and then not provide it with an opportunity to empty itself. A dog doing its best to be clean in the house may become constipated or may be unable to adhere to its training. The fault does not lie with the dog but with an inconsiderate owner.

Obesity

Just as an unsuitable but convenient diet coupled with a lack of exercise is making our own species increasingly obese, dogs too are becoming more so. To allow a dog to become obese should be regarded as a form of cruelty that gives rise to a number of serious and potentially fatal conditions. An extensive survey (A.T.B. Edney and P.M. Smith, 'Study of obesity in dogs visiting veterinary practices in the United Kingdom', *Vet. Rec.*, 5 April 1986) showed that 24.3 per cent were obese, and of these 2.9 per cent were gross. Labradors were found to be the breed most likely to become obese and both neutered males and females were shown to be more likely to become so than were entire dogs. The problem has become so widespread that, as with our own species, the market is now inundated by proprietary slimming diets. Again, as with our own species the solution lies in eating less and exercising more.

An overweight, obese or gross dog will be very greedy, soliciting food at every opportunity. It will tend to sleep and refuse to walk more than a short distance and so cannot take part in even the least demanding activity. Warm weather will make him pant excessively and his appearance will excite the pity of owners whose dogs receive a better standard of care. An obese dog will be inclined to develop arthritis, diabetes, heart disease, a reduced level of liver function, impaired digestion, a reduced resistance to disease and will tend to have an appreciably shorter lifespan than a fit dog. At the lowest level, keeping the dog alive, will involve the owner in considerable veterinary fees as well as an increased expenditure on food. Reducing a dog's weight is simply a matter of reducing its intake of food and of ensuring that everyone who may be inclined to give the dog any food is aware of the importance of not doing so. Reducing the intake to about two-thirds of what would be required for a dog of normal weight, soaking food to increase bulk without increasing calorie content and feeding several small meals each day will help to assuage hunger. Avoiding all titbits and, in extreme cases, making use of specialist prescription diets will also help to reduce the weight. Once the loss of weight inclines the dog to be more active its level of exercise can be gradually increased.

Timing

When during the day a dog it is best to feed a dog is dependent on when it is exercised and on the household routine. Dogs tend to excrete shortly after they have been fed, but, in normal circumstances, what they pass are the remains of the previous day's meal. If it is convenient to do so, they should be fed out of doors and remain there until they have passed their motions. Feeding might be followed by leisurely exercise but it is unwise, particularly in the case of large and deep-chested dogs, to allow them to exercise vigorously. Some of these breeds are subject to bloat, more correctly referred to by veterinary surgeons as gastric dilation-volvulus (GDV), that is often precipitated by vigorous exercise immediately after a meal but the aetiology is unclear and the condition may also occur at other times.

If a dog is involved in competitive activities or is away from the house when it would normally be fed it is wise to provide it with a meal at or close to the normal time. This will avoid the possibility that the dog may learn to associate competition or an excursion with going hungry and so incline it towards resenting these activities. If the dog tends to be car sick the feed should be given well before the journey is likely to begin and should, perhaps, be reduced in quantity, with the remainder being given when the journey is complete.

8 Behaviour

When I carefully consider the curious habits of dogs
I am compelled to conclude
That man is the superior animal.

When I consider the curious habits of man
I confess, my friend, I am puzzled.

Ezra Pound, *Meditatio* (1916)

Introduction

Although Charles Darwin had a deep interest in dogs, one which drove his father to tell him in a forthright letter that, 'You care for nothing but shooting, dogs, and rat-catching, and you will be a disgrace to yourself and all your family', he only used what this interest had taught him to produce incidental comments on the theme to which he was devoting his attention at the time. It would be perfectly feasible to support the suggestion that the first tentative steps towards the study and understanding of canine behaviour took place in 1872, with the publication of Darwin's *The Origins of Expressions of the Emotions in Man and Animal*, and even after more than 130 years it is difficult to think of any text on ethology that is so thoroughly researched and so interesting to read. Even so, the palm should really go to Konrad Lorenz whose work during the early decades of the twentieth century laid the foundations for the modern study of the science and led to a popular interest in the behaviour of dogs.

The understanding of canine behaviour revolutionized the way in which dogs were trained. It ceased to rely on dominance reinforced by punishment and instead relied upon understanding supported by reward. Further work by Nikolaas Tinbergen, who like Lorenz became a Nobel Prize winner, Eberhard Trumler and the popular writer Michael Fox produced a greater interest in the new science. Not all its practitioners adhere to scientific principles and some are patently exploitive, but more and more is being learned that not only helps to understand this behaviour and to use this knowledge in order to train dogs in a far more humane and productive manner than hitherto, but also provides the means by which owners can derive greater enjoyment from their relationship with dogs.

Until a few years ago most scientists would have dismissed as anthropomorphism the suggestion that dogs and other animals might be capable of feeling pleasure. The fact that dogs reacted in ways which seemed to indicate pleasure at the return of their owners or some other person after even a brief absence tended to be dismissed as evidence that the dogs were feeling pleasure. The reaction of a dog to the caress of its owner or even of another dog also tended to be founded on something less reliable than objective scientific observation. The very idea that dogs and other animals might be capable of feeling emotions was almost a taboo subject among researchers who dismissed the possibility that, while they could experience fear, pain, joy and anger, were incapable of more complex emotions such as embarrassment, pleasure, love and grief. Even without support from the Vatican it seemed that Descartes' baleful influence has not totally disappeared.

Marc Bekoff faced the subject in 2000 when his *The Smile of a Dolphin* explored the way in which animals responded to certain stimuli. He pointed out that Jaak Panksepp's work at the University of Ohio showed that young rats responded to being tickled by emitting high-pitched sounds not dissimilar to laughter. Panksepp suggested that they were experiencing pleasure and was promptly accused of anthropomorphism by his fellow scientists. The criticism was refuted when it was discovered that animals at play produced opioids, the same chemicals produced by humans who are experiencing pleasure. The research received support from Michel Cabanac's work on reptiles. Then, at the beginning of 2004, reports were published of work carried out at the Neurosciences Institute in San Diego by Ralph Greenspan and Bruno von Swinderen. This conclusively demonstrated that even fruit flies were capable of learning and that, in its turn, may suggest that they are capable of an emotional range far greater than had previously been expected.

The accumulated research seems to go a long way to supporting the observations made by owners who interpret the behaviour of their dogs as demonstrative of pleasure or enjoyment. Once again, the observations and interpretations of dog owners have been shown to be ahead of those of expert scientists. However, there is still room for more work to be done, not least to see whether or not there are significant differences between breeds that could influence their relative popularity.

Although comparisons between breeds have not yet been undertaken, the negative aspects of the behaviour of pedigree and mixed breed (mongrel) dogs examined in 1987 among 2,334 American owners found significant differences between the two groups. The study revealed that pedigree dogs were more inclined to bite, chew, soil the house, be unruly and marginally to be more inclined to shyness. Mixed breeds, on the other hand, were found to be more inclined to bark, be carsick, chase cars, eat faecal material, eat non-food material, dig, escape, be fearful of noise, be a finicky eater, steal food, beg for food, jump on people and furniture, fight, kill other animals, be overprotective, run away and whine. The balance was slightly restored in favour of mixed breeds because more of these were reported as presenting no problems than pedigree breeds. The same survey also compared obedience-class trained dogs with dogs with no formal training and found that in those categories likely to be affected by training obedience-trained dogs scored better than those without formal training. Barking, begging, jumping on people and furniture, fighting with strange dogs, house soiling, unruliness and whining were all significantly reduced.

A dog should be respected for what it is – a dog – and not be called upon to act the part of a surrogate child, with all the attributes of a child. Some breeds have been bred to look like very young children, with large, round heads, large eyes, short limbs and plump, rounded bodies, but, no matter how far this process may have been taken by breeders. they are still dogs. Much is made by some of the new breed of behaviourists of the fact that dogs are descended from wolves and so are best understood by reference to the behaviour of them. The fact that some wolves were prepared to modify their behaviour and accept a degree of domestication, coupled with further modification which has taken place during 100,000 years of selective breeding, must have diluted wild behavioural patterns to the extent that some have disappeared while others are now no more than vestigial. Selective breeding has also changed the appearance of domestic dogs in such a way that about 5,000 recognizable breeds now exist. The largest of these are up to a hundred times bigger than the smallest. Such a variation would be unsustainable in the wild, and, if variations in length of leg, head proportions and length of back are also taken into account, it becomes apparent just how far domestic breeds have diverged from their wild ancestors. One aspect that is not revealed by cursory examination is that the brains of domestic dogs are about 20 per cent smaller than that of a wolf with a similar skull size. Does this mean that domestic dogs are less intelligent than wolves? Are pariah dogs that live by their wits more or less intelligent than domestic breeds? If they are, might this give some credence to the unsupported belief that mongrels are more intelligent than pedigree breeds? Certainly domestic dogs, while retaining some vestigial remains of wolf-like behaviour, have jettisoned many behavioural characteristics of their wild ancestors. Healthy wolves do not attack people except in self-defence or in defence of their young; their customary means of defence is flight, and so, as far as threats to the safety of people are concerned, the ravening wolf is almost entirely imaginary. However, over many thousands of years domestic dogs have largely lost their fear of people and so may be as much inclined to attack as to flee.

Ill-conceived breed-specific legislation inspired by the Dangerous Dogs Act tends to equate the gladiatorial breeds with attacks on people. The evidence refutes this misguided supposition, but, even if it were soundly based, the legislation unjustly targets some breeds but not others. The simple facts are that any dog with teeth is capable of biting, but that few do so, and children are far more likely to be injured or killed by their own parents than by dogs.

From the 1960s psychiatrists and psychologists developed new means to treat disturbed and mentally limited people. The theories were adapted in order to develop the means to treat canine behavioural problems and this spawned a number of self-styled behaviourists, not all of whom were deeply immersed either in the basis of behaviourism or in dogs. They tend to make great play of the biological relationship between domestic dogs and wolves and use this to support theories that purport to explain behavioural characteristics. As inevitably as with the latest diet fad or must-have fashion accessory, as more people give the matter a little informed consideration the fashion will disappear along with its predecessors. Not all wolves contributed to the development of domestic dogs. Those that did so were probably atypical. During something like 40,000 generations it is inevitable that selection by man, the effects of breeding from a limited population, would tend to have as great an effect on wolf-like behaviour as it has had on physical appearance.

Wolves like being within a pack of related animals. Most domestic dogs are condemned to a solitary existence, only the fortunate few have the opportunity to live with others of their kind and to develop the sorts of relationship that characterize their species. A wolf pack is a hierarchical unit in which a dominant female and her mate not only control hunting expeditions but also are the sole breeding pair within the pack. Their position is attained and maintained by their superior physical and mental attributes. Only the dominant, alpha pair will breed, though others in the pack will help to rear their young and so allow the dominant female to resume her place in the pack's hunting expeditions quickly. Domestic dogs, both male and female, are promiscuous, and will usually mate with others with which they have no social relationship. Dogs in a household may develop into a pack and may recognize a dominant individual. They will howl in unison, much as do wolves in order to maintain auditory contact with one another, although they may also howl in order to express their misery. Dog owners may unintentionally and may be encouraged by some behaviourists and trainers to interfere in the pack hierarchy.

Early attitudes to dogs were often informed by a moralistic abhorrence of the total lack of shame with which they indulged in public displays of procreation and defecation. Their lack of shame gave rise to the belief that dogs lacked morals and, as a consequence, they were often subjected to religiously inspired criticism. The attitude is now perhaps less prevalent because our own former behavioural standards have become more relaxed.

Aggression

Aggression is the most common reason given for dogs being euthanased. Any dog that bites a person should be regarded as a potential danger. Even so, man is far more likely to be attacked and injured or even killed by one of his own species, even by a family member, than by a dog.

There can be no acceptable mitigating circumstances that excuse a dog for biting someone. Any overt display of aggression in a show dog may result in the Kennel Club's banning that dog for life from all shows as well as refusing to register its offspring.

Unless dogs can mix harmoniously with others, with other animals and with people of all ages they are a liability to their owners and to society in general. If an owner is incapable of curbing any tendency towards aggression the only sensible solution to the problem lies in euthanasia.

Barking and Howling

In spite of repeated assertions by 'experts', Basenjis are not the only breed of dog that do not bark. Nor are dogs the only animals that do so. According to the *National Geographic* website, 'Elephants eat roots, leaves, grasses and sometimes bark.' Experts also suggest that domestic dogs have been taught to bark. When, why and how they were taught is not discussed. Shakespeare appreciated the cry of hounds 'match'd like bells, each under each'. Gervase Markham recommended that hounds should be matched 'into three equal parts of Musick, that is to say, Base, Counter-tenor and Mean'. Izaak Walton appreciated 'what music doth a pack of dogs then make to any man, whose heart and ears are so happy as to be set to the tune of such instruments!' But Joseph Addison probably best expressed the enjoyment to be had from the cry of hounds, which 'by the Deepness of their Mouths and the Variety of their Notes, which are suited in such Manner to each other, that the whole Cry makes up a compleat Consort'.

Wild dogs do not bark but are capable of a wide range of vocal sounds – howls, growls, grunts, whimpers, squeaks, squeals included. With few exceptions, all breeds of domestic dog bark and none are mute. Primitive domestic breeds, including the Basenji and the New Guinea Singing Dog, do not bark, which is not to say that they are mute. They are capable of making a variety of sounds in order to communicate. When, how and why domestic dogs learned to bark, whether they have regional or breed-specific accents has been little studied and are beyond the scope of this book. Dogs vocalize in order to facilitate communication. They may bark in order to draw attention to their presence or to the presence of interlopers in their territory. They may bark in greeting or out of sheer exuberance. Howling may be an expression of misery, a means to advertise their presence to other members of the group or even a greeting to a new day. Grunts are most often a sign of contentment while growls may be either playful or threatening. Whines and whimpers may be a means to seek attention, an invitation to play, a sign of submission, a greeting or an indication that the dog is in pain. Dogs should not be denied the opportunity to vocalize, although in excess this may not endear them to neighbours or even to all members of the household. But in countries in which rabies is endemic caution must be exercised if the tone of a dog's customary barks changes.

Body Language

Dogs communicate with one another and with their owners – if their owners are bright enough to understand – less by means of voices but by body language. The signals are often subtle and may be confused by someone not well versed in dog language. Puppies reared in isolation until they are twelve weeks old may never develop an ability to communicate with other dogs or with people, they are seldom trainable and as companions are more likely to be a liability than an asset. The importance of socialization based on a variety of early experiences is further underlined.

Very young puppies will nuzzle and paw their dam in order to solicit food and will later lick her mouth to try to persuade her to regurgitate food for them. They may perform the same action with their owners who may interpret this as 'kissing'; little do they realize what is expected of them. As the puppies develop, they will learn to solicit play from their littermates or from friendly adults by lifting a paw or lowering their forequarters. The actions will persist and will be recognized throughout life.

Introduced into a strange environment, especially one in which dogs are present, a dog may react in one of two ways. It may stalk, ears and tail raised and with an air of confidence, into the environment, or it may revel its fear by lowering its head and quarters and tucking its tail under its belly. If the dog is very fearful it may demonstrate its submissiveness by rolling on its back and displaying its underbelly. Whether a dog with heavy pendulous ears or one with no tail has the ability to communicate reduced is a matter for debate, but, since the basic signals derive from a creature with very mobile ears and tail, the possibility cannot reasonably be dismissed out of hand. Furthermore, a dog's tail makes important contributions to its ability to communicate not just with its owner but also with other dogs.

When dogs meet for the first time or after even quite a short separation, they will indulge in a ritual that involves the dominant animal smelling the anal and genital parts of the inferior dog. The most powerful scent glands are situated around the anus. A dog may even go so far as to urinate on the inferior dog and especially if it is a bitch.

Boredom

Professor David Morton of the University of Birmingham has suggested that anthropomorphism may be a good starting point for recognizing the likelihood of boredom in dogs: if someone believes that the situation in which a dog is kept would be boring, it is reasonable to assume that the dog may also

A confident but not aggressive posture …

Supplication.

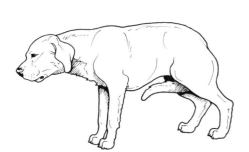

A fearful posture.

Invitation to play.

An abject, submissive posture.

Soliciting play.

find it so. In order to relieve the boredom, the dog may indulge in destructive or self-damaging behaviour, become noisy or attempt to escape. The solution to the problem is to be found in providing the dog with companionship, with stimulating exercise and an opportunity to play and with toys to suit the situation. Even a radio or television may help to ward off boredom, no matter how execrable the programme!

Coprophagy

Owners tend to regard eating faecal material as an objectionable habit. Dogs, for their part and assuming that they are capable of having such a point of view, may find some of the things that people eat equally offensive. Only because owners find the habit distasteful is it necessary to find the cause and try to affect a cure.

The cause may be any one or a combination of boredom, acquired habit, dietary deficiency or a simple liking. Wild canids remove their puppies' faeces from the nest as a means to maintain a degree of cleanliness as well as to reduce scents that may attract predators, and by licking their offspring's' anal regions stimulate the passing of faeces. Domestic bitches, given the opportunity, may do the same. The greatest problem with coprophagy is not the distaste it induces in fastidious owners, but in the fact that the faeces of other dogs, as well as of cats, foxes, rabbits, sheep and other animals may contain the eggs or larvae of harmful parasites.

The addition of iron rich supplements to the diet is said to have a deterrent effect by making the faeces less palatable, but admonishment, perhaps reinforced by a startling diversionary activity, may also be effective.

Dreaming

Sleeping dogs will often twitch and squeak

1: alert and confident; 2: suspicious; 3. warning; and 4. aggressive.

Dominant behaviour does not necessarily involve aggression.

in a way that suggests that they are dreaming, and so, the experts assure us, they are. However, very young puppies will exhibit precisely the same behaviour, but what experience has a young puppy had that will provide material for dreams?

Facial Expressions

Dogs have a wide variety of facial expressions some of which are most often found in particular breeds but most of which are common to all breeds whose physiognomy enables them to make the expression. Dalmatians sometimes contort their faces into something which resembles both a grin and a snarl and which can only be interpreted by taking other signals into account (*see* below). It has to be remembered that facial expressions derive from those produced by a wolf, a creature with a long but broad and strong muzzle, slanted, forward facing

eyes and small, erect ears. Dogs with very different characteristics may not easily produce expressions that other dogs can readily interpret.

Wild canids and the range of expressions they use are based on the fact that all have eyes that face forward. Some domestic breeds have eyes set on the side of their heads. To what extent this detracts from their ability to communicate by means of facial expressions has not yet been thoroughly studied but such a departure from the norm cannot be without some effect no matter how trivial. A confident dog will face the object of its attention and focus both eyes on it; ears will be pricked and facing forward. Only the nose will move, twitching restlessly as it takes in information beyond the range of our ability to detect let alone comprehend. The dominant dog will invariably outface its inferior which will often turn its head to one side. The inferior dog will lower its ears almost to a horizontal position. Again, the extent to which this position if normal in some breeds restricts their ability to convey their anxiety has not yet been fully studied. The confident expression may also turn to one of suspicion if anything untoward is detected. The ears will be only partially raised and the eyes narrowed.

A snarl conveys some degree of threat, a warning rather than an invariable precursor to aggression. The ears will be slightly lowered, they eyes narrowed and the teeth exposed by drawing the lips. A snarling dog may also strut about, emphasizing its size and confidence and may be silent or reinforce its apparent displeasure by means of a prolonged guttural rumble; but one that is doing no more than expressing its displeasure at the unwanted attention of very young puppies may simply stand, making no attempt to leave them to their own devices, and snarl.

A number of breeds grin to produce an expression that may be mistaken for a snarl by those who are not familiar with the subtle differences between the two expressions. Darwin, in *The Origin of Expressions and Emotions in Man and Animal*, described, perhaps for the first time, the canine grin that appears to be confined to a small number of breeds. Dalmatians, Schnauzers and Dobermanns appear to be most inclined to grin, though whether the tendency is inherited or learned is debatable. The expression differs from a snarl in that it is invariably directed at people and seldom, if ever, at other dogs. The lips are withdrawn and the muzzle becomes wrinkled but the teeth are not exposed as with a snarl.

Fear

Analysis conducted by the American Guide Dogs for the Blind revealed that loud noises, machinery and other animals are the principal reasons for fear in dogs The treatment they receive during puppyhood is the most likely cause of these fears and may also produce a fear of people. A kindly upbringing, allied to gentle exposure to a variety of experiences is by far the best way to instil in puppies the confidence they need to cope with potentially frightening situations later in life. If, as a result of some unfortunate experience, an adult dog becomes fearful of some situation or object, the road back to normality may be long and difficult, demanding patience and understanding from the owner. In extreme cases it may be necessary to subject a dog to sedative medication, but this should be regarded as a last resort. Other causes of fear will be discussed under individual headings.

Fighting

Dogs, even those that are not usually aggressive, may fight for many reasons. They may fight in order to defend themselves, their companions, their owner, their territory or their possessions. Bitches in season may become quarrelsome. All dogs may become jealous of the attention given to or sought by other dogs.

There are almost as many recommended ways of separating fighting dogs as there are dog owners. Each method may work in certain circumstances but not in every case. By restricting a dog's breathing, perhaps by twisting its collar, using its lead as a ligature or by pinching its nose, it might be forced to relinquish its hold on its adversary. Care must, however, be taken to ensure that it is not deprived of air so as to render it unconscious or that it does not become the victim of a retaliatory attack by its adversary or that it does not turn its attention to the person who has released its hold. Some owners advocate pouring water into the dog's mouth, or go even further to argue the case for immersing both dogs in water. Others suggest that twisting the tail will distract it, and some even recommend inserting a finger into the dog's anus. If the dogs are small enough, lifting them off the ground by the hind legs may result in the hold being released and the dogs' swinging away from one another. A similar effect might be achieved by hanging one on each side of a gate or a fence. People involved in dog fighting use what they refer to as 'breaking stick' in order to prise a dog's mouth open; these dogs are strong and their hold tenacious but breaking sticks are effective.

The chosen method will depend on the circumstances in which the fight is taking place and on the size and determination of the combatants. Pulling fighting dogs apart – which is likely to cause far more damage than the fight itself – should never be used as a means to separate them. Nor should those who are invoked in the attempt to separate them add to the excitement of the occasion by shouting or screaming. Measured calm is the order of the day, although this is not easily maintained when a dog is being severely hurt by an adversary and when there is a strong chance that one or both dogs might turn on the mediator. Most dogs will continue a fight until one or other has decided that enough is enough, and at this stage will display signs of submission, but by this time both dogs may have sustained more or less serious injuries. The gladiatorial breeds may in some cases provide an exception to this general rule. They may be psychologically incapable of displaying or reacting to signs of submission and may fight to the death.

Frustration

Every breed of dog was developed in order to fulfil some particular purpose. That purpose may have been no more demanding than to provide an animated fashion acces-sory, but in other cases may have required the dog to put its life at risk. Sight hounds are bred to chase quarry and, deprived of this function, may well relieve their frustration by chasing something else. Several breeds, not just sight hounds, will relieve their frustration by chasing cats, cars, cyclists and postmen. They need, if only for their own safety, to be persuaded not to do so. Herding breeds deprived of the opportunity to herd sheep may chase cattle, horses or other livestock, some will herd poultry. This sort of behaviour does not endear the dogs or their owners to those who own the objects of this misplaced attention. A farmer is entitled to shoot a dog if that is the only way that he can protect farm stock from its unwelcome and potentially damaging attentions. The dog's owner will be liable for any damage done by his dog and will probably find that the injured livestock is far more valuable than might have been imagined.

It is often suggested by those who have not given the matter a moment's thought that terriers, because of their former subterranean employment, are inclined to dig. Not all terriers, of course, were so employed. Some hunted vermin above ground, some were gladiators. Those breeds that were employed to evict foxes, badgers and otters from their underground retreats followed them into what Fleming described as 'their lurking angles, darke dongens, and close caves'. The holes into which the existing occupants had already dug, terriers ventured; terriers did not dig them. Why then should terriers inherit something that was not required of them? In fact, any bored dog will dig, simply to relieve its boredom or in search of edible roots and other material.

Hackles

Along the top of their neck and over the

Working terriers may live, play and work as a unit.

withers, many breeds have a growth of longer coat that in some breeds is referred to as a ruff, but more generally as the hackles. If the dog finds itself in a disturbing situation it may raise these hairs in order to make itself look larger and more threatening. A threatening facial expression, a raised tail and a stiff-legged walk may augment the appearance created by raised hackles.

Isolation Anxiety

Some dogs rely so heavily on the continual presence of their owner that they react to being alone in ways that cannot be tolerated in a normal family household. This anxiety may manifest itself in destructive behaviour, biting, chewing and scratching household furniture and fittings, incessant barking, whining and howling, defecation and urination and efforts to escape from their confinement. Although some of the symptoms may be similar, isolation anxiety should not be confused with the behaviour of a bored dog left alone for long periods.

The behaviour appears to have some degree of breed-related bias, but is most often encountered among mongrels obtained from welfare kennels. No studies appear to have been done to discover whether the dogs were discarded by their previous owners because of this behaviour or whether the behaviour is a product of their experience in kennels. Dogs appear to be most inclined to exhibit the symptoms of isolation anxiety if, after they have been accustomed to the continual presence and attention of their owner, they are suddenly deprived of these. If puppies are accustomed to spending some period alone during the day, they are likely to accept periods of isolation when adult. Smaller breeds can be confined in a cage that they regard as their own, while larger breeds can be given access to their bed. All might appreciate being left with a familiar toy and the sound of a radio or television.

Juvenility

Some breeds, particularly among what used to be called lapdogs and are now less accurately described as toys, have been deliberately engineered in order that they should look and behave as much as possible like a human child. This has perhaps been taken furthest in Pugs whose sleek coats, short fat limbs, short tails, rounded bodies, large rounded heads and large, rounded, forward-facing eyes are all intended to reproduce the appearance of a human child. In the eighteenth and the nineteenth century the process went even further and the entire earflap was cut away in order to make the shape of the head even closer to that of a human child.

All very young puppies tend to have similar features, even those breeds which, as adults will have heavy coats, long slender limbs, long tails, pointed muzzles and sharply pricked ears, as neonates present a very different appearance. These breeds may be less independent and more reliant on their owners than others. The tendency also enhances their dependency, that some owners persist in regarding as evidence of 'love'.

Marking

All canids, both wild and domestic as well as numerous other species, make use of the scent given off by urine in order to advertise their presence, mark their territory and declare their proprietorial claim. They will do so within what they regard as their own territory, especially when potential usurpers invade it. To ascribe the behaviour to cleanliness or the lack of it is to indulge in a degree of anthropomorphism that betrays a failure to understand. Some zealous local authorities have even gone so far as to make the dubious assertion that urine marking at the foot of concrete streetlights rots the concrete and makes the structure dangerously unstable.

RIGHT: Territorial marking.

BELOW: Receiving messages from other dogs that have passed this way.

Sleeping under the duvet may be frowned upon by some behaviourists, other accept it as part of cementing a bond.

Neurosis

Neuroses in dogs are often learned as a consequence of poor socialization as very young puppies, either as a result of a traumatic incident later in life or from the behaviour of a neurotic owner. The dog may have a single symptom or he condition may be more generally manifested in displacement activities such as barking, house soiling or overexcitement. Treatment consists of reassurance and the withdrawal of rewards for neurotic behaviour.

Nibbling

Also sometimes referred to as 'flea biting', nibbling is a normal greeting, perhaps indicative of a greater degree of pleasure than is signalled by sniffing or licking. Dogs will nibble another's neck. The habit appears to be stimulated by the presence of hair, which is perhaps why dogs will nibble the faces of bearded owners but lick the faces of those who are beardless. The habit may be a hangover from the cleansing of newborn puppies and grooming them as they grow older. It is a habit that dogs share with most other social animals, including our own.

Oestrus

Entire bitches normally come into season twice a year although some toy breeds and others may do so every four months, while primitive breeds, like their wild cousins, may do so on an annual basis. Although most bitches will develop a regular cycle and owners can eventually predict with some degree of accuracy when they are likely to come into season, this may be disrupted by contact with other bitches in season – what breeders often refer to as 'the me-too syndrome' and vets as synchronized oestrus – by weather conditions, by having produced a litter at the previous season or by some illness or malfunction.

A pronounced swelling of the vulva followed by a blood-infused discharge that will eventually clear usually signals the onset of oestrus. Some bitches may swell only slightly and others may have an almost imperceptible discharge, while others may swell considerably and produce a copious discharge that will stain anything she happens to rest on. Even during these early stages of oestrus the bitch will be very attractive to dogs and so should be kept well away from any possible suitors, some of whom may arrive unannounced from a considerable distance, having been attracted by the pheromones she will be excreting. The bitch will lick herself and will deposit small drops of urine as visiting cards in what she regards as suitable places. This behaviour may pass unnoticed and may even disguise her condition from all but the most observant owner. She may begin to arch her back and displace her tail, if she has one, to one side when she is stroked or being groomed or in the presence of dogs, other bitches and even the family cat. At this stage the bitch is at her most fertile and is likely to make determined efforts to attract or find a suitable male. She should be kept in strict seclusion until all signs of being in season have disappeared and then, if only for good measure, for a few days more.

Bitches usually ovulate about ten days into their season, but a particularly observant owner may notice small signs that would pass unnoticed by others. Thus the onset of oestrus may be counted from different points in its progress. Some bitches may ovulate later in their season than others and eggs may be retained for a number of days during which, if allowed access to a dog, they may conceive. It therefore pays to err on the side of caution.

Pica

Pica, the depraved ingestion of unnatural items of food, is probably the product of an instinctive attempt to rectify some deficiency of bulk or nutrition in the diet. The efforts are unlikely to be successful and may lead to the eating of indigestible or poisonous material. Dogs that have a well balanced diet are unlikely to exhibit this behaviour.

Phobias

As sentient creatures, dogs can, like ourselves, surely be expected occasionally to harbour irrational fears. They may share with us phobias about people in white coats, but may not fear spiders or birds, but they may fear gunfire, fireworks, aerosol sprays and the like. Again like people, dogs may have an intense dislike of certain people or dogs, as well as of the creatures they have been bred to harass such rats and foxes. They may even respond to and reflect their owner's fears, dislikes and phobias.

No detailed investigation intent on discovering whether certain breeds have a predisposition to developing phobias – to thunder, passing vehicles, household appliances, fireworks, gun shots and the like – has been carried out. The government is currently being persuaded to enact legislation that will afford some degree of protection against the inappropriate use of fireworks, but it seems unlikely that a phobia about fireworks will exist in isolation from other phobias to loud and unexpected noises. Such legislation would be welcome, not just for dogs, the vast majority of which, if properly socialized, react with indifference to the noise, but for people of a nervous disposition and as a means to curb the behaviour with which fireworks seem to be often associated. Someday a behaviourist will explain why so many dogs react strongly to the use of a vacuum cleaner or a long brush, although whether the reaction can be classified as a phobia is open to doubt; do dogs dislike vacuum cleaners and long brushes or do they regard them as playthings?

The veterinary treatment of behavioural problems (Robin Walker, 'Common canine

Destruction is often an indication of boredom.

behavioural crises', BVA Congress, 1999) has in recent years moved on from recommending euthanasia to increased reliance on proranolol (a beta-blocker) and phenobarbitones, coupled with the education of owners. However, by far the best way of avoiding the difficulties associated with phobias is to acquire puppies and adults that have been reared in a situation in which they were not exposed to a wide variety of experiences. Dogs reared in kennels, no matter how clean and well appointed, may well grow up to be perfectly happy in a kennel environment but may prove incapable of adjusting to life in a busy household. During their early weeks of life, puppies need to become accustomed to the conditions in which they are expected to live as adults. Households sights and sounds, the television and radio, the noise of the washing machine and the vacuum cleaner, the activity associated with the routine of a busy household all contribute to the process of socialization that is essential to produce well-adjusted family dogs. The critical period during which puppies seem best able to absorb and be conditioned to new experiences appears to be between the ages of five and ten weeks, after which they become progressively less able to make the adjustments required if they are to become trouble-free companions.

All breeds have been bred for some particular purpose that, even years after its original purpose in life may no longer be appropriate, impinges on their behavioural characteristics. The denial of ingrained behaviour may lead to aggression.

Dogs are social animals and may be inclined to panic if they become separated from the group, whether this is seen as their owners or another dog. Panic may take the form of destructive behaviour, determined attempts to escape or unrelenting noise. A dog that is lost may avoid capture and even show signs of having wiped its memory clean of any recollection of its owner. Such dogs appear almost to be reverting to a wild or at least a feral state. Once more, it is important to ensure that dogs have been carefully and well socialized and that they have the necessary confidence to accept periods of loneliness without being unduly disturbed.

Scenting

Dogs seem to find the smell of fox excrement and long dead animals particularly attractive. Their owners seldom share their attraction to the musky, pervasive smell and to that of decomposing cadavers. Whether dogs roll in fox excrement in order to mask their own scent or as the canine equivalent of Chanel No.5 is debatable. There appears to be no effective way of breaking the habit; resignation, supported by understanding and a sense of humour, may be the best attitude for an owner to adopt.

Scooting

Scooting refers to a tendency of some dogs to drag their anal regions along the floor or ground. The behaviour is often associated with attempts to ease the discomfort caused by anal gland problems, but it may also be associated with perivulval eczema, particularly in bitches with infantile vulva or which are obese. The possibility also exists that scooting is used to scent mark.

Sexual Frustration

Wolves live in a society in which only the dominant pair will mate and breed. Domestic dogs are bred with a more promiscuous attitude to sex. A stud dog is expected to be willing to mate bitches with which he may be unfamiliar, and bitches are expected to accept the advances of a strange dog readily. Most companion dogs, having been bred to be far more promiscuous than wolves, live a life of total celibacy. Many, however, live within sight, sound and smell of potential partners but are denied access to them. The combination of increased promiscuity with loss of opportunities to mate cannot be expected to do anything other than lead to sexual frustration. Such dogs, both entire and castrated, may mount and go through the motions of mating other dogs of the same sex and all manner of unsuitable objects, from people, furniture and toys, to the cat and the legs of a chair. This sort of behaviour may be embarrassing for owners but its main importance is that it reveals that the dog is enduring a degree of frustration.

The obvious way to relieve this is to enable them to breed; but unless the dog is of suitable quality relieving frustration cannot be justified by producing substandard puppies. The remaining options include training and neutering.

Shame

Because dogs have no reservations about copulating or defecating in public view (behaviour that our own species can no longer claim to be free of), it has been suggested that they lack the ability to feel shame. This suggestion is reinforced by the fact that dogs are incapable of blushing. Mark Twain wrote in *Following the Equator* (1897), 'Dogs are incapable of blushing, a fact, which has given rise to the suggestion that, they are incapable of shame. Even if dogs could blush this would pass unnoticed on a black dog.

Man is the Only Animal that Blushes. Or needs to.'

'Sixth Sense'

Dogs are often credited with a sixth sense that enables them to accomplish all manner of surprising things. It is claimed that the have a premonition of earthquakes, thunderstorms, death and of the imminent return of family members. At least some of these may have perfectly reasonable explanations that have not yet been fully investigated or understood. Others may on closer and objective examination prove to be the product of the imagination of fond owners.

Sleep Preparation

Experts appear to be unanimous in their belief that dogs turn round in a tight circle before they settle down to sleep. They tell us that this behaviour is not only intended to create a comfortable bed but also to check for the presence of nearby predators. In fact, the behaviour is not universal since many dogs never behave in this way. Some will do so only as a prelude to whelping, when the urge to create a nest seems to be at its strongest. Others may scratch their bedding into a rumpled mess, and some of those who sleep on paper have been known to energetically shred it, but few go in for this procedure of turning round.

Perhaps dogs have discarded the habit and what is now left is a mere shadow in the collective expert memory. Perhaps some dogs have learned that their beds are not made more comfortable by turning round in them and that they have no need to check for the presence of predators. Perhaps the habit is confined to some breeds and is not found in others. The experts insist that canine behaviour is inherited from wolves, but do wolves turn round before they sleep? Darwin discussed the idea in his *The Expression of the Emotions in Man and Animals*:

> Dogs, when they wish to go to sleep on a carpet or other hard surface, generally turn round and round and scratch the ground with their fore-paws in a senseless manner, as if they intended to trample down the grass and scoop out a hollow, as no doubt their wild parents did, when they lived on open grassy plains or in the woods. Jackals, fennecs, and other allied animals in the Zoological Gardens, treat their straw in this manner; but it is a rather odd circumstance that the keepers, after observing for some months, have never seen the wolves thus behave.

Observations made by H. N. Bessel during C. F. Hall's *Polaris* expedition in 1871 suggested that Eskimo dogs never turn round before lying down, because, it was suggested, 'for countless generations, [they cannot] have had an opportunity of trampling for themselves a sleeping place in grass'. In fact, as any observant owner will quickly realize, dogs do not invariably curl up to sleep. Observations carried out on two Arctic breeds (Stuart Winterton, private correspondence, 2004) suggests that Alaskan Malamutes turn round before settling down, both in their beds and elsewhere. Greenland Dogs, formerly called Eskimo (Esquimaux) Dogs, never turn round but simply drop down once they have selected a place in which to rest. What Trumler (*Understanding Your Dog*, Faber & Faber, 1973) described as the 'hearthrug' position involves the dog in lying with its rear and its front legs extended. A third position involves the dog lying on its side with both its rear legs extended to one side and the fourth involved the dog lying on its back with slightly curled spine and legs drawn up. The last three are most likely to be seen when the dog is warm, confident and relaxed while the first is adopted if the dog is cold or ill at ease.

It is interesting to watch a dog becoming drowsy. His eyes will be partially closed and his head will nod as sleep gets closer. If the dog is not relaxed, this process may be prolonged until he decides to find a more appropriate place in which he can sleep undisturbed.

Spinning

Some dogs that spend the most of each day closely confined in a small cage or kennel may develop a habit of running round and round in small circles. They may exhibit this behaviour even when they have complete freedom to run and play. Much the same sort of behaviour is to be seen among zoo and circus animals that are deprived of freedom or a stimulating environment. The behaviour must not be confused with the restless circling sometimes indulged in by aged dogs.

Tail Chasing

Some dog owners are amused by the fact that their dog chases its tail and may, by praising it and encouragement, teach it to perform the routine on command. No harm is done if the owners also teach their dog to stop chasing its tail when told to do so. Once physical reasons such as anal irritation have been eliminated, reasons must be sought in the way in which the dog is kept. An objective assessment is likely to reveal that its environment is not sufficiently stimulating and that tail chasing derives from its frustration.

Travel Sickness

Some dogs, like some people, suffer from motion sickness during even quite short car journeys. This may have some physiological basis that can be treated with veterinary medicines. Others may be travel sick as a nervous reaction to the experience. If puppies are taken for short rides in the car and fed when they return, they will not only be less likely to be sick during the acclimatization period but will also begin to associate a car ride with reward. Some breeds seem inclined to dribble incessantly during such journeys. They do not vomit but copious quantities of saliva do nothing to improve the comfort of other occupants of the car. In these cases medication may be the only feasible solution; but this cannot be employed on dogs that will later in the day be involved in competition because of its soporific effect.

9 Injuries and Ailments

When a dog looks unkindly in his coat, though he has been physicked, give him three doses of powdered glass, as much as will lie heaped up on a shilling to each dose. This will make his coat very fine, and he will look well in his skin; besides it is a very great cleanser. The powdered glass must not be made of the green glass bottles, but from broken decanters and wine-glasses, powdered and ground in an iron mortar, then sifted through a fine muslin sieve.

Col George Hanger, *To All Sportsmen, and Particularly to Farmers and Gamekeepers (1814)*

Introduction

The purpose of this chapter is not to alarm nor deter but to inform. Most of the conditions described here are rare and have never been encountered by dog owners of many years' standing. A wise choice of breed and breeder and a good standard of care will help to avoid many of the rest, but accidents will happen and it is as well to be prepared in order to relieve the dog of unnecessary suffering by recognizing the first signs if ill health and to deal with them before they become intractable, either by simple treatment by the owner or professional treatment from a vet.

Veterinary Surgeons

Wise breeders will insist that one should never use a vet whose waiting room plants have died. A good vet with knowledge of and more than a professional interest in dogs is a pearl of great price. Unfortunately these are not only few and far between but tend to be found among the older generation. One manufacturer of a popular

---

Useful Facts

It is useful to know the ranges within which the most readily available indicators of a dog's condition should be:

Body temperature:	38.3–38.7°C (10.9–101.7°F)
Pulse rate:	70–100/min
Respiration rate:	15–30 breaths/min

---

brand of food alarmingly claims that: 'Dogs need regular veterinary care. Simply put, their lives depend on it. If your dog hasn't been to the vet in the past twelve months for recommended vaccinations and a check-up, please make an appointment today.' This is both blatant commercialism and arrant nonsense. If your dog is fit and well, what purpose is served by taking it for a veterinary examination? Routine vaccinations apart, a healthy, well cared for dog may go through a long life without any need to visit a vet.

If a puppy is bought locally the breeder will be able to recommend a good vet as well as to warn against those who are less good. If the puppy has not been bred locally, it is not difficult to seek advice from experienced dog owners, particularly those who breed or compete with their dogs. Price should be regarded as secondary to service, but by shopping around the vets in the area it is a simple matter to compare prices for a standard service such as vaccinations. Fees vary from area to area depending heavily on the cost of premises and staff, but within the same area there is less reason for wide variations to exist, although exist they undoubtedly do.

In recent times the profession's reputation has taken some damaging punishment as a result of the actions of a tiny minority who have destroyed the cosy image created by James Herriot. The profession has also been hit by the recession in the agricultural industry which has meant that farmers are now less likely to consult a vet than was formerly the case. Vets have also lost income as a consequence of the loss of their monopoly to prescribe and supply a number of medicines now readily and economically available from specialist pharmaceutical outlets. It is far more economical to use such things as wormers and insecticidal products bought from a specialist supplier than from a vet.

Vets as a whole get most of their income from the owners of companion animals, the majority of these being dogs, and thus it is not unreasonable to expect a vet to understand and take an interest in the activities in which dogs and their owners are likely to become involved.

Genetic and Congenital Disorders

In 1987 the European Convention for the Protection of Pet Animals, drawn up by the Council of Europe, catalogued a number of conditions it regarded as inimical to the welfare of pet animals, including dogs. Some of the proposed prohibitions were long overdue but others were simply risible. It was proposed that 'surgical operations for the purpose of modifying the appearance of a pet animal or for other non-curative purposes shall be prohibited and, in particular, the docking of tails, the cropping of ears, devocalization and declawing and defanging'. Docking is already illegal in Britain, unless carried out by a veterinary surgeon, the cropping of ears has been banned for over a century, devocalization would certainly be regarded as cruel as would defanging, but the removal of dewclaws from puppies is still carried out by many breeders in order to prevent future injury and inconvenience and as a cosmetic procedure. It was further and more contentiously proposed that maximum and minimum heights and weights should be set for dogs, that maximum values for the relationship between height and length should be set and that limits for the shortness of the skull should be set. It was also suggested that breeders should prevent the occurrence of persistent fontella, abnormal positions of the legs, abnormal size and shape of eyes, very long ears and folded skin. In addition, breeders should discontinue the breeding of dogs carrying semilethal factors, recessive-defect genes, hair-lessness and merle colouration.

It is undoubtedly true that a loss of contact with the original purpose for which breeds were developed has removed the guidelines imposed by function, but the clock cannot be turned back to enable dogs to hunt wolves, to bait bulls or engage in combat one with another. It is also true that an increased regard for what are considered to be attractive features and to advances in veterinary science which enabled puppies with exaggerated features to be born, survive and reproduce has meant that puppies carrying deleterious exaggerations and which would previously have died have crept into many species of companion animals, including cats, rabbits, birds and fish. It is not surprising, although it is certainly regrettable, that dogs must also be included in the list. In 1974 the Kennel Club, working with breeders through their breed clubs, completed an exercise that was intended to modify any requirements that might have crept into breed standards and which might be deleterious to welfare. The exercise was less stringent than some had hoped would be the case but it had to balance what might have been regarded as desirable with what was possible. The exercise is continuing. Some of what the Council of European proposed may be desirable but some is certainly impossible and unnecessary. It is perhaps significant that, while it frowns on small size and persistent fontella, both of which are ascribed to Chihuahuas, that is among the breeds that have the longest life span. After more than seven years since the proposals were first published no significant progress has been made towards their implementation.

As living creatures, dogs, like us, may inherit conditions injurious to their well-being. That will always be the case, but the best breeders individually, through their breed clubs and through kennel clubs, continually strive to reduce the incidence of inherited disease. Even so, it has to be realized that not all can ever be eliminated, either from dogs, our own or any other species. The completion in 2002 of the map of the canine genome revealed that man and domestic dogs share about 360 such diseases. Seven-foot-tall basketball players, seven-stone jockeys and bald men all suffer from genetically transmitted abnormalities. Anyone who set out to breed basketball players or jockeys would choose abnormally tall or abnormally light parents. The same is true of dog breeders. Great Danes are bred from abnormally tall parents and Chihuahuas from abnormally small ones. It is wrong to assume that all abnormalities are necessarily undesirable. It is also quite wrong to assume that genetic defects are to be found only in recognized breeds. Mongrels and, perhaps to a lesser extent, cross-breeds also carry and may transmit undesirable genetic characteristics. Poor standards of care coupled to survival of the fittest may result in the early death of the worst affected individuals, but the fact remains that all domestic dogs may carry and transmit inherited abnormalities and diseases.

Over 1,000 dysmorphic syndromes have been identified in man and these are only a fraction of the genetic abnormalities identified thus far. Poor eyesight, deafness, heart defects, susceptibility to assorted diseases and about 4,000 other genetically transmitted conditions have been identified. About 400 have been identified in domestic dogs. The Kennel Club facilitates the testing and recording of potential breeding stock as part of its fight against genetically transmitted diseases. It promotes research into the way in which these are transmitted and thus enables breeders to plan breeding programmes that will reduce and eventually may eliminate many genetic disorders. Some of this work is directly beneficial to man. It would be salutary to be able to quantify the value of this work in economic as well as health terms, but, to whatever degree, the fact is that this is yet another way in which dogs contribute to society. Caring breeders already make use of the weapons now available, but it is likely that some form of compulsion will be necessary in order to prevent breeders with lower standards promulgating inherited defects.

At the beginning of 2004 the Kennel Club, the Animal Health Trust and the British Small Animal Association initiated a nationwide survey of purebred dogs. This was carried out among the 70,000 breed club members through the United Kingdom. The aim was to identify important disease conditions in British dogs by examining the frequency of disease in different breeds, identifying important breed-specific problems in order to improve the success of control schemes and identifying future research priorities. The survey is perhaps the biggest step yet undertaken to record and improve the health of pedigree dogs. It will also assist prospective owners to make informed decisions about their choice of breed. However, the survey will not provide additional information about the health or otherwise of mongrels, cross-bred dogs or unrecognized breeds. The absence of any reliable information should not, however, be regarded as evidence of freedom from disease.

Pain

Signs that it is suffering some degree of pain or discomfort may provide the first indication that a dog is unwell. Different breeds have different levels of tolerance to pain and may exhibit subtly different symptoms. When they are in pain, working terriers, especially when their concentration is focused on their quarry, seem almost impervious to pain. The gladiatorial breeds may

also be disdainful of it. Some dogs will react to a vaccination or the insertion of a microchip implant as though they were being murdered, others remain totally unconcerned. It is tempting to wonder to what extent the treatment they receive and the signals they receive from their owners affect their reaction. A study carried out in 2001 divided the perceived responses to pain by dogs into ten categories, each of which was further subdivided (L. Holton *et al.*, 'Development of a behaviour-based scale to measure acute pain in dogs', *The Veterinary Record*, 28 April, 2001):

- Demeanour: anxious, depressed, distressed, quiet.
- Response to people: aggressive, fearful, indifferent, sullen.
- Response to food: disinterested, eating hungrily, picking and rejecting food.
- Posture: curled, hunched, rigid, tense.
- Mobility: lame, slow/reluctant, stiff, stilted, unwilling to rise.
- Activity: restless, sit/lie down, sleeping.
- Response to touch: crying, flinching, growling, guarding, snapping.
- Attention to painful area: biting, chewing, licking, looking, rubbing.
- Vocalization: crying, groaning, howling, screaming, whimpering.
- Physiological signs: tachycardia (rapid heart beat), panting, tachypnoea (rapid respiration), pyrexia (feverish), salivating, trembling, muscle spasms, dilated pupils.

In addition to this catalogue, observant owners will notice that a strained expression, unusual ear carriage, shivering, depressed tail carriage and an overall hangdog demeanour may also provide indications that the dog is in discomfort.

For the present purpose, it is sufficient to divide the canine illnesses into three broad categories:

• Those inherited or present at birth, in other words genetic or congenital (these pose no threat to any other creature unless the dog is bred from, in which case its genetic defects may be transmitted to its offspring and its tendency to congenital defects may also be transmitted);
• second, some conditions may be produced by inappropriate standards of care, such conditions cannot be transmitted from dog to dog;
• third, some diseases may be acquired from another dog and, less frequently, from some other creature.

Preventive Procedures

Prevention is, of course, preferable to cure, but procedures, particularly those involving surgery, which aim to avoid conditions that might better be avoided by a good standard of care need to be considered with care both in terms of their intended effect and their possible side effects. Although some of the original reasons used to justify non-thera-peutic surgery have long been discredited, the procedures themselves may be justified on other grounds and may still be practised.

Vaccination

In 1816 Lt Col Peter Hawker, author of *Instructions to Young Sportsmen*, received a let-ter signed *Canis Amicus* which recom-mended vaccination as an effective means to prevent distemper. The writer said that,

about two years ago, in Sussex, I had fre-quently heard at table, that inoculating a dog with cow-pox virus would prevent it from having the distemper. About half year afterwards, having a pointer puppy, a few months old, I inoculated it. ... I should observe, the part where I inoculated my dog was on the inside of the foreleg, under the

shoulder. Cutting a very small place with a pair of scissors, and rubbing the bone, or quill, charged with the virus, into the wound, did it. From the appearance of the wound, a few days after, I was afraid the virus had not taken effect, but I have been told that this slight appearance is usual.

Hawker gave the suggestion a more exten-sive trial than was represented by a single dog, and by 1832 was able to report that 'so little, if any, has been the effect of distemper after it, that I have not lost a dog since the year 1816'.

For more than just a few years dog own-ers, both in Britain and in the United States, have been questioning recommended vacci-nation regimes. The majority of owners are reasonable, responsible people who want to do their best for their dogs while avoiding unnecessary expense. They do not want to expose their dogs to the possibility of side effects, no matter how remote, which may arise as a consequence of the overuse of vaccines. They are obliged to rely on profes-sional veterinary advice and their vets choose to rely on what they are told by pharmaceu-tical companies. Both vets and pharmacists are commercially involved, perhaps even commercially reliant, on increasing the use of vaccinations. It would not be in any way surprising if both groups were to seek to maximize the income they receive as a result of the use of vaccination. Pharmaceutical firms have already sought to protect their profits by using the courts in order to try to prevent Third World countries from gaining access to cheap generic drugs; recommend-ing unnecessary vaccination regimes would demonstrate a not totally dissimilar attitude.

The advent of vaccines that owners could confidently regard as reasonably safe and effective has occurred during the lifetime of many existing owners. Not all have forgotten the time when vaccines could, and sometimes did, give rise to the very diseases against which they were intended to confer protection. Some produced side effects that, from time to time, had something more serious than mere cosmetic effects. In 1988 it was revealed that a distemper vaccine produced encephalitis in some dogs; all ten cases examined at Glasgow University were euthanased. Other studies in Iceland revealed that antibodies produced by distemper vaccines could persist for six to seven years and were often still present four to five years after vaccination. The findings gave support to the practice adopted by many experienced owners to have puppies vaccinated, but not to have annual or biannual boosters. It was not surprising that some owners were reluctant to take advantage of the benefits vaccines had to offer and looked around for other forms of protection. Some of these may have provided no effective protection at all, but the widespread use of conventional vaccination slowly reduced the threat of disease. Those who chose not to protect their dogs by the use of vaccination were, in effect, benefiting from the responsible attitude of those who were more conscientious.

Breeders who remember the advent of canine parvovirus will also remember its effect on puppies and older dogs. Many puppies died within a matter of hours, others were left with heart and other defects that remained with them for the rest of their lives. The scourge was brought under control only after safe and effective vaccines became available. Dog owners now have access to a range of vaccines that provide protection against several life-threatening diseases. However, they do occasionally still give rise to harmful side effects and may not always confer full protection. Anecdotal evidence accumulated and did so against a background of the reluctance of pharmaceutical firms to address the concerns of their cus-

tomers. Independent scientific evidence not only exposed the danger of vaccinating dogs that were already immune but also demonstrated that the recommended intervals between vaccinations failed to take account of the duration of immunity. An inappropriate regime that recommended too frequent vaccination increased the sales of vaccines by manufacturers and veterinary surgeons, but may have been unnecessary if not harmful. Marketing techniques became aggressive, ranging from harshly worded 'reminders' to pressure on local authorities to insist that boarding kennels must require all boarders to have been vaccinated within the preceding twelve months.

PETS (the Pet Travel Scheme) was introduced as a replacement for the system of quarantine that had kept Britain effectively free of rabies virtually throughout the twentieth century. It enabled companion animals, principally dogs, to travel freely throughout Europe and was subsequently extended to the Canada and the United States. The scheme is based on the need for travelling animals to be vaccinated against rabies and other diseases and to have been wormed within a stated period prior to the journey. The advent of PETS enables dog owners to travel overseas and to acquire, far more cheaply than is possible in Britain, a number of medicaments, including vaccines. If these are not properly stored they are likely to become useless or even dangerous. Following a report by the Veterinary Products Committee (VPC) Working Group on Feline and Canine Vaccination, it became apparent to all who cared to see that existing recommendations were not credibly sustainable. Not all chose to see. Some organizations with international reputations chose to regard the report as a vindication of the benefits of pet vaccination, something that had never seriously been questioned. They chose, however, to relegate recommendations that vaccination regimes should make use of risk assessment in order to take account of different levels of threat from different diseases, in different localities and in different breeds to a lowly place among the VPC's recommendations. They chose also to downplay the fact that the lack of validity of the old, broad-brush approach to vaccination had been demolished. Some pharmaceutical manufacturers have taken a very different attitude. They appear to be in the vanguard of manufacturers who have responded to the VPC's recommendations. Intervet's published statement is unequivocal:

We'll no longer focus on the minimum period of 'guaranteed' protection, and instead study the actual duration of immunity. It means we'll stop treating all vaccines as the same, and instead realize that some provide longer immunity. Above all, it means we recognize that every owner has a choice. That unless we are completely open – with all the latest facts about adverse reactions, disease prevalence and duration of immunity at our fingertips – we may never see their animals again.

Outmoded regimes are reinforced by the insistence of boarding kennel licensing authorities that all dogs must have been vaccinated within the previous twelve months. There are no exceptions for dogs that may have been blood-tested and been shown to have adequate immunity. There are no exceptions that recognize the use and possible value of homeopathic vaccines and there are no exceptions that recognize the right of owners to refuse to have their dogs vaccinated. The attitude of these authorities is not based on logic or sound science. Are unvaccinated children refused a place in schools? Why do they insist that immune dogs must be revaccinated? Why do vaccination regimes in Britain and North America

differ for products produced by the same pharmaceutical companies? What evidence exists that demonstrates whether or not homeopathic remedies produce immunity? Dog shows and other competitive events do not insist on vaccination yet appear not to be a significant source of infection. Neither the Kennel Club's General Code of Ethics nor those of most breed clubs regard vaccination as a sine qua non. Why do some vets insist that puppies previously vaccinated by another vet should undergo another course of vaccination? Are some vaccines incompatible with others? Do some vets distrust the documentation provided by other vets? Not even the recently introduced PETS scheme requires that dogs that travel to or from Britain be vaccinated other than against rabies. It seems that the risk assessments carried out by the Kennel Club and by the former Ministry of Agriculture before the introduction of PETS did not show that unvaccinated dogs were a risk to others or were themselves at significant risk.

Many owners continue to follow the regime that has served them well for many years. Puppies receive their initial vaccinations, but that is the end of it. This has been the prevailing situation these many years past, not just in Britain but in many others too. The epidemics, which vets and pharmaceutical companies predict, have not materialized. However, any reduction in the level of immunity in the dog population as a whole could create ideal conditions for an epidemic to develop. The salient factor is not whether dogs have been vaccinated recently, but the level of immunity within the dog community. While it is at a high level, epidemics will be kept at bay; when it falls epidemics become more likely. Research carried out by Swedish vets in Iceland revealed that immunity following a single course of injections could last well into a dog's old age. A report of this research was published in *The*

Veterinary Record. Neither pharmaceutical companies nor vets have published any dissenting views. The British Small Animal Veterinary Association (BSAVA) Scientific Committee went so far as to admit that there is a 'possibility that we are vaccinating too frequently'. The Swedish investigation reflects experience in North America where vets from the College of veterinary medicine, Auburn University have accepted that 'a protective immune response may persist for years following vaccination, making routine administration of annual booster vaccines unnecessary'.

The American Kennel Club has funded an investigation into the persistence of distemper adenovirus type 2 and parvovirus immunity in order that the value of booster vaccines can be evaluated. There appears to be no similar investigation being carried out in Britain.

Complaints received by the Suspected Adverse Reactions Surveillance Scheme (SARSS) revealed that before 1997 adverse reactions attributable to vaccines were running at about 20 per cent of all complaints; in 1998 the figure rose to 32 and to 38 per cent in the following year. The number of reported adverse reactions resulting from veterinary treatments represented a tiny fraction of the whole and it is probable that only a very small percentage of adverse reactions give rise to reports. The fact that the number of vaccine-related reactions is far greater than those produced by any other procedure must raise cause for concern.

Immunity is conferred as a result of the production of antibodies responding to the threat of disease provoked by natural exposure or by vaccination. Antibodies are produced as a reaction to a perceived threat. Immunity depends on antibody titre levels. When these fall below a certain level, the dog is susceptible to disease; while they are high the dog is protected from that disease

or from a particular strain of it. Blood tests are able to provide the means to identify antibody strains and measures levels, but are appreciably more expensive than a single vaccination.

Puppies receive some degree of immunity across the placenta and, soon after birth, from the colostrum fleetingly present in their dam's milk. Thus orphan and other hand-reared puppies may lack sufficiently high levels of natural immunity to provide adequate protection. Immunity may be-come progressively less and may have dis-appeared by the time the puppy is eight weeks old or it may persist for up to sixteen weeks. To what extent it may be prolonged by contact with immune companions is uncertain. It is doubtful whether bitches that are not themselves immune can confer immunity. Until reliable evidence is available about the efficacy of homeopathic treatment it cannot be regarded as an alternative to vaccines.

At eight or ten weeks of age, when their own immune system has developed well enough to produce antibodies, puppies usually receive their first dose of vaccine. If maternal immunity has then disappeared, the first vaccination will restore their immunity, but if maternal immunity remains the vaccine will have no effect, some even suggest that vaccinating on top of maternal immunity may have a deleterious effect on the immune system and may produce other adverse reactions. The best course might be to withhold vaccination until a blood test demonstrates that maternal immunity has fallen below the level at which it might interfere with conferred immunity.

The usual, and cheaper, British option is to give a second dose of vaccine about one month after the first. In the USA the recommended protocol involves vaccination at six to eight weeks followed by repeat vaccinations every three or four weeks until the puppy is between fourteen and sixteen weeks old. Thus the protocol could involve as many as four separate vaccinations. The puppy is then regarded as being immune, but its immunity is seldom measured. The developing American protocol differentiates between CORE and NON-CORE vaccines. CORE vaccines, routinely given to all puppies and repeated every two or three years, cover distemper, parvovirus and rabies. NON-CORE vaccinations are only given to dogs that may be exposed to a substantial risk of infection. The infections in this NON-CORE group include tracheobronchitis, leptospirosis, coronavirus enteritis, giardis and Lyme disease. Are American dogs more or less healthy than their British counterparts as a consequence of less frequent vaccinations? Pharmaceutical firms and some vets in Britain continue to recommend that vaccination should be repeated every twelve months, although some vets are now adopting a regime that relies on revaccination only every three years. The first International Veterinary Vaccines and Diagnostics Conference in Madison, Wisconsin also recommended the protocol.

Questions arise: can a bitch that is not herself immune transmit maternal immunity? What are the short- and the long-term effects of vaccinating a puppy that retains maternal immunity? Can immunity be conferred by contact? Is it necessary or even desirable that the initial course involves two vaccinations? How long can vaccine conferred immunity be expected to last? Why do vets not make more routine use of blood testing? Is the protocol recommended by pharmaceutical firms in concord with the National Office of Animal Health's Code of Practice for the Promotion of Animal Medicines (May 2000)? Is it professionally ethical for vets to recommend treatment that may be unnecessary?

Apart from the possibility that the present protocol may not be the best as far as canine health is concerned, the debate among owners and some vets raises the thought that it is fuelled more by commercial interests than by concern for disease control. The thought may be a long way from the truth, but, unless vets address it by demonstrating that they have considered other protocols, it can only damage their reputation. The *Journal of the American Veterinary Medical Association* put the matter succinctly: 'If revaccination at intervals longer than one year results in adequate protection from disease, then annual revaccination is not optimal, and less frequent revaccination would be an appropriate goal.'

Quarantine

The 2004 Woolridge Memorial Lecture given by Lord Williamson of Horton examined just some of the many oddities of EU decision-taking. While stressing the need for greater emphasis on the stewardship of the countryside and rural communities, Lord Williamson argued the need for a 'much harsher, fully justified' system of frontier controls to protect individual countries against the import of human and animal diseases. He indicated the systems of controls that exist in the USA, Australia and New Zealand as preferable to the lip-service paid by the EU to preventing the cross-border spread of disease.

Although Lord Williamson was principally focused on farm animals, what he had to say was equally applicable to companion animals. The system of quarantine which had kept Britain free from rabies for over 100 years has recently been abandoned for potential vectors imported from countries certified free of the disease. Quarantine had two major advantages: it worked and those who brought dogs into Britain paid for it. Its disadvantages were that it was inconvenient and costly for those who wanted to bring dogs into Britain; by separating dogs from their owners it created stress for both. However, quarantine was not merely an effective means of defence against rabies, it also provided protection against a number of other diseases and parasites. Some of these are zoonotic and could pose a considerable threat to public health, the treatment of which would add to the problems already experienced by a hard-pressed National Health Service.

Countries in eastern Europe already have far from impervious border defences, even though in some of them rabies remains endemic and is likely to remain so for the foreseeable future. Countries in southern Europe harbour reservoirs of parasites some of which are not yet found in Britain. Some of these have been kept at bay by quarantine and by a climate that was inhospitable to them. The system of vaccination, health checks and documentation on which importing is supposed to be dependent is suspect. Britain's border controls are flimsy and over-extended. In some European countries it is not difficult to acquire documentation without undergoing the tests and checks that make it valid. Adequate defences would be inconvenient for travellers and costly to the public purse. Even then they would be incapable of detecting animals infected with internal parasites. Quarantine has disappeared and the climate is becoming progressively warmer and more to their liking. It is only a matter of time before companion animals throughout Britain are infected with conditions that threaten their health and the health of those who come into contact with them.

Once the companion animal population is infected the cost of treatment will fall on owners, but the costs of treating people who have been infected would fall on the National Health Service. Human disease and the costs of treatment could foster public antipathy to companion animals. If a flimsy defence allows diseases to cross the channel (if by some good chance it has not already done so), the political reaction will not be to improve the defences or eliminate the diseases – it will be to eliminate the carriers of that disease.

In a letter to *The Veterinary Record* of 8 May 2004, Gerald Coles of the Department of Clinical Veterinary Science, University of Bristol, drew attention to the need for improved disease control as the most important issue in improving the animal welfare. In particular he identified the most important diseases of dogs as those caused by parasites but said that 'there are no awards for research into parasites and their control'.

DACTARI, the body set up by DEFRA to investigate the occurrence of exotic disease in dogs, during it first operative twelve months identified eleven cases of Leishmaniasis, seven of babesiosis and four of ehrlichiosis. The Department of Health is being kept informed and the Advisory Committee on Dangerous Pathogens taking an active interest. 'These results, says DACTARI, 'confirm that travel or residency abroad is a significant risk factor for dogs being infected with exotic diseases.'

The problem is not a new one. Dogs and fleas have a long and well-documented symbiotic relationship but this has recently been aggravated by the freedom, introduced by PETS, for dogs to travel overseas and for dogs resident overseas to come to this country. Surveillance techniques are rudimentary or non-existent and thus almost wholly ineffective. Some are species-specific but others affect animals other than dogs including people and give rise to diseases that are difficult to diagnose, problematical to treat and which may cause lasting harm to patients.

More people, especially children, and more dogs are injured in their own home than anywhere else. Dogs, like very young children, explore novel materials with their mouths. They have no alternative and so never grow out of nor be trained to stop doing so – chewing trailing electric wiring, plastics and children's toys. All owners should have a basic knowledge of what substances are harmful to dogs and enough knowledge to mitigate their worst effects. The best remedy, however, is the obvious one: treat dogs as inquisitive children and ensure, as far as possible, that they cannot harm themselves by gaining access to dangerous appliances or substances.

Zoonoses

Zoonoses are those diseases carried by animals and which can be transmitted to man because of their unusually close physical contact with man; cats and dogs are probably the greatest sources of infection though man may also be infected by diseases carried by poultry, cattle and, indirectly, by a number of wild species. Badgers are held by some to be a major source of tuberculosis in cattle; tits and crows infect bottled milk with *Campylobacter*, and collared doves are heavily infected with Chlamydia. The recent incursion of Daubenton's bats carrying the rabies-like Lyssavirus has caused the death of one man and represents a continuing and possibly growing danger.

The risk of zoonoses which have not previously been seen in Britain has been increased by the introduction of the PETS travel scheme, which enables people to travel to and return from parts of the world in which these zoonoses are endemic. During the first four years after the introduction of PETS, when it was largely confined to Europe, 48,329 dogs came into Britain, the majority returning to this country, but some were being imported. Of these almost 7 per cent failed the checks. The potential for importing exotic diseases is strong and has become stronger with the acceptance of animals from North America and Canada.

Specific Conditions and Diseases

Abrasions
Not normally a problem because dogs are usually protected from abrasions by their sense of balance and their coats.

Abscesses
A localized infection often caused by a puncture wound or the presence a foreign object; cleansing the wound is important, but, if the dog develops a fever, treatment with antibiotics may be required.

Acanthosis nigrans
Thickening and blackening of the skin; treat with antiseptics and in chronic cases with corticosteroids. The condition seems to be particularly associated with breeds with short coats and dark skins.

Acariasis *see* Mites

Addison's disease: *see* Hypoadrenocorticism

Aelurostrongylus abstrusus: *see* Lungworm

Ageing
Advertisements aimed at our own species attempt to convey the impression that the appearance of ageing, if not ageing itself, can be delayed by the use of cosmetic substances. Dogs lack the gullibility that might tempt them to believe such claims. In fact, ageing is inevitable and its symptoms largely unavoidable. Some breeds, especially the heavily bodied ones, may begin to show signs of ageing at five or six years and may have a life expectancy of no more than seven or eight. Other breeds may remain active and in good health until their mid-teens and even longer. Good standards of care will help to prolong active life.

Allergy

Dogs may become hypersensitive to a wide range of household cleansing agents. The usual symptoms are tender and reddened skin, pruritis and self-inflicted trauma arising out of attempts to relieve irritation. By far the best treatment is the identification and removal of the allergen.

Alopecia

The loss of hair may be induced by hormonal imbalance as well as ringworm and trauma. Some bitches routinely develop bare patches of skin over the ovaries at certain stages in their oestrus cycle. When all other causes have been eliminated, it may be necessary to undergo a course of hormonal injections.

Anal glands

These two small sacs are situated just below and to each side of the anus. Their purpose is to produce the scent with which individual dogs mark their presence. Studies of wolves have shown that the secretions are strongest in dominant dogs and are stimulated by the presence of an unfamiliar male. They serve much the same purpose as does aftershave and other scented products among males of our own species. If the dog's diet contains insufficient roughage, and sometimes when it does not, the sacs may fill and produce irritation and discomfort that the dog may seek to relive by scraping its anus along the ground. If untreated, the sacs may become impacted and need veterinary treatment, but it is a simple, if unpleasant, procedure for an owner to check and empty the anal sacs on a regular basis. If the base of the tail is lifted and curled over the dog's back the anus will be exposed. The thumb and forefinger can then squeeze from below the sacs towards the anus and so express the contents, which may be ejected with some force. It is therefore prudent not to stand behind the dog while the sacs are being emptied!

Anal adenomata

Characterized by multiple, pale-coloured, firm lumps around the anus. Veterinary treatment is necessary.

Anal furunculosis

Inflammation of the anus, giving rise to licking and abscesses. Mostly found in German Shepherd dogs and may be inherited.

Anal sacculitis: *see* Scooting

Anaphylaxis

Hypersensitivity to trauma, vaccination, injuries giving rise to vomiting, diarrhoea, collapse and possibly death.

Anterior uveitis

Dull and thickened iris, lacrimation often secondary to another ocular disease.

Arthritis

Gives rise to excessive joint wear, pain and lameness. Veterinary treatment is indicated.

Ascarid infestation

See Roundworm.

Ascites

A distended, fluid-filled abdomen may indicate chronic liver disease. Veterinary treatment is indicated.

Aspergillosis

Produces copious nasal discharge, emaciation and weakness. Confirmation and treatment of the diagnosis by a vet is necessary.

Ataxia

Inco-ordination.

Babesiosis
Also called tick fever and now making its appearance in Britain as a result of infected dogs being brought into the country.

Balanitis
Swollen and red prepuce accompanied by discomfort and irritation, treatment with antibiotics is indicated. Attention to cleanliness will help to prevent the condition.

Blindness
Old age, accidents or inherited conditions may give rise to partial or total blindness. If hearing and, perhaps more importantly, the acute sense of smell remains intact, a blind dog may manage very well especially on familiar territory. The behaviour of a blind dog, its general demeanour will be little different from that of a happy and contented dog.

Bloat
Gastric dilation-volvulus (GDV); large and deep chested breeds may suffer from bloat; the dog will initially show signs of discomfort and the stomach will rapidly become distended. If the dog's life is to be saved it is essential that veterinary treatment to relieve the condition be carried out expeditiously. The aetiology is not fully understood but the condition appears to be associated with overeating, especially when followed by vigorous exercise. Gastric haemorrhage and ulceration, hypotension and electrolyte disturbances may all contribute to a high mortality rate. Caring breeders of those breeds prone to bloat will make buyers aware of the problem and provide details of how best it may be avoided.

Bordetella bronchiseptica
Kennel cough; one of several bacteria that cause chronic bronchitis and pneumonia and normally resident in the respiratory tract of dogs, pigs and humans. A persistent, dry, rasping cough is characteristic but seldom give rise to long-term problems, except in puppies and aged dogs. Associated with distemper.

Brucellosis
Caused by *Brucella canis*, a bacterium as yet not found in Britain but endemic in the southern USA, Central and South America and some mainland Europe countries. The bacterium gives rise to late abortion in bitches and to infertility in dogs. The infection can be transmitted to man in whom it gives rise to chronic, flue-like symptoms. Even the most stringent surveillance of imported dogs is unlikely to detect all those carrying the infection.

Bursitis
Swelling of the joints found mainly in heavy dogs that lie on hard surfaces. Prevention consists of providing soft resting places, but chronic cases may require surgery.

Campylobacteriosis
Diarrhoea caused by a zoonotic bacterium. Antibiotic treatment is indicated.

Canine distemper
Before the advent of effective vaccines it was generally accepted that puppies would have to 'go through' distemper, resulting in the death of a high proportion of them and permanent damage to some of the survivors.

Canine adenovirus, Types 1 and 2
Kennel cough; as far as dog owners are concerned the difference between the two types of cough is almost academic. Type 1 is mainly transmitted as a result of contact with urine passed by an infected dog; puppies are at their most vulnerable when maternal immunity has declined and for a week or two after they have received

protective vaccines. Most adult dogs recover from infection quickly, but may then shed infection for up to nine months. Kennel cough is thus highly infectious and vaccination is essential if dogs are at all likely to come into contact with any infectious animals – while at exercise, at shows or by contact with visiting dogs.

Canine hepatitis
Rubarth's disease; a highly infectious condition arising out of infection of the liver, leading to fever, depression, vomiting, abdominal pain and corneal oedema and giving rise to the characteristic 'blue eye'. Infection may result in the death of untreated puppies and aged dogs.

Canine parvovirus infection
Infection can be fatal to young puppies; symptoms include depression, anorexia, vomiting, diarrhoea and dehydration. Infected puppies may recover but with residual cardiac problems.

Cataract
Opacity of the lens of the eye caused by cataracts may develop as a result of injury or as a secondary product of another eye disease. Old dogs may develop blue or greyish eye coloration as a consequence of old age. Cataracts in their inherited form may develop in juveniles, in mature dogs or in aged animals, all of which may be genetically different. Senile cataract is far less common in dogs than in man.

Cheyletiella infestation
Mite infestation that produces dry, scaly skin, irritation leading to self-inflicted damage and pruritis. The mites are very small and obvious only to keen observation or microscopic examination.

Chronic liver disease: *see* Hepatitis

Cleft palate
A condition in which the palate is split and which may be congenital or inherited. It may repair spontaneously but the need for surgical intervention is likely. Puppies with cleft palates may not thrive. The condition tends to occur most frequently in both its congenital and inherited forms in brachycephalic breeds.

Coccidiosis
A diarrhoeic condition, especially in dogs housed together in ill-ventilated conditions.

Congestive heart failure
A condition, probably congenital, that gives rise to breathlessness, a dry cough, rapid, weak pulse, enlarged liver, pale and swollen mucous membranes. Veterinary treatment is necessary.

Conjunctivitis
Symptoms include reddened conjunctiva, discharge and irritation. Often caused by allowing a dog to put its head out of a moving car's window. The condition is easily treated using an eye ointment, but is far easier to prevent with common sense.

Constipation
Characterized by hard stools difficult to pass and giving rise to pain. Produced by a diet with inadequate roughage. Treat with a liquid paraffin enema and add bran to the diet.

Convulsions
May be produced by the effect of some poisons, eclampsia, distemper, tetanus and rabies. If any doubt exists as to the cause, veterinary advice should be sought.

Corneal oedema
Early hepatitis vaccines often gave rise to 'blue eye', a condition in which the cornea

goes blue; may also be caused by hepatitis infection. The condition may persist for some time but will clear spontaneously.

Corneal ulceration
Infection of the cornea or the presence of foreign bodies may give rise to a persistent discharge and opacity. Treat with antibiotics.

Cough: *see* Kennel cough

Cryptococcosis
A fungal infection that produces nasal discharge, persistent cough, nervous incoordination, wasting and blindness. The outcome is likely to be fatal.

Cryptorchidism
An inherited condition in which one or, more rarely, both testicles fail to descend into the scrotum. At the BSAVA Congress in 1988 Albert Dorn voiced his opinion that 'the veterinary profession must regulate and control dog shows and exhibitions to restrict the entrance of affected dogs'. A survey (D. Yates *et al.*, 'Incidence of cryptorchidism in dogs', *Vet Rec.*, 19 April 2003) revealed that the incidence in cross-bred dogs (mongrels and cross-breeds?) was 3.9 per cent and in pedigree dogs 8.7 per cent. Of the breeds examined, Chihuahuas had the highest incidence (30.4 per cent); Boxers (20.6 per cent) and German Shepherd Dogs (14.0 per cent) were also abnormally high. Retained testes produce an increased risk of tumours and fail to induce hormones that produce secondary sexual characteristics; consideration should be given to surgical castration. Dogs with one retained testicle may be fertile. The condition may give rise to testicular neoplasia, torsion with associated pain and necrosis. Every Kennel Club breed standard contains a stipulation that 'male animals should have two apparently normal testicles fully descended into the scrotum'. Many exhibitors would prefer that such dogs were banned from competition, as is the case in most other countries. The testes are usually fully descended at birth or shortly afterwards. Any puppy that has not got two fully descended testicles by the time it is ready to go to its new home should be regarded as a potential cryptorchid.

Cystitis
Bacterial infection giving rise to frequent, painful urination and incontinence for which antibiotic treatment is necessary.

Deafness
Deafness may be the product of trauma, infections, drugs, poisons and old age, and may be inherited, in which case it is most frequently associated with white, merle, harlequin or spotted coloration. Advancing years may bring deafness with them and some dogs of any age may develop a selective deafness in order to ignore commands. They seem oblivious to even the most stentorian instruction but can hear even the faintest rattle of a food dish from a considerable distance. It is arguable that deaf dogs are more severely handicapped than blind ones – a blind dog will still respond to commands but a deaf one cannot be expected to respond to something that cannot be heard. During the early stages of hearing loss dogs may still respond to high-pitched sound such as a whistle or to vibrations, but may not show symptoms other than what may be regarded as disobedience to summons. As the condition develops, they will bark less and in a different timbre than formerly, their ears will be less mobile and they may sleep more and be less easily roused. Most will adjust to hand signals, although these are only of use if the dog can see the signals. Buyers should seek assurance that the chosen puppy is not deaf and should carry out a few simple tests, by watching its response to sounds, to verify

this. Ear infections or carbon monoxide poisoning may also cause deafness.

Dehydration

Every dog should have constant access to clean water. Dogs that are fed on dry, complete diets need far more water than those which have a diet, tinned, moist or home prepared that contains a substantial amount of liquid.

Demodectic mange

A parasitic infection, also called follicular mange, producing skin lesions, waxy dandruff, pustules and hair loss. Treat with appropriate medicaments.

Dental calculus

An accumulation of brown plaque on the teeth. Some dogs will tolerate having this removed by the owner, but the best treatment consists of prevention by using hard food or toys. The condition of itself is trivial but may give rise to gum disease and bad breath. *See* also Teeth below.

Depraved appetitive: *see* Pica

Dermatitis

Caused by bacterial, fungal or parasitic infection, especially in skin folds, and self-inflicted trauma arising out of anal gland infection. Characterized by hair loss and reddened and thickened skin.

Diarrhoea

Diarrhoea is most often a symptom of some other condition, but is, in its own right, a threat to a dog's welfare, especially to puppies or to aged dogs. Even a short bout may dehydrate a dog very quickly. Further debility is produced by loss of appetite, coupled with the inability to utilize nutrients. The colour, smell, consistency and frequency of motions are all indicative of the underlying problem. Yellow or greenish, watery, sour smelling stools are suggestive of an unusual degree of bowel mobility. Small, frequent stools passed with difficulty are indicative of colitis. Large stools suggest malabsorption or a disorder of the small bowel. Tarry, black stools suggest bleeding in the upper digestive tract, bloody stools indicate bleeding in the lower bowel and pale stools are suggestive of liver disease. Watery stools suggest extreme activity and irritation of the bowel wall, possibly arising out of poisons or severe infections. Large, light coloured stools, greasy, smelling of food or with a rancid smell indicate digestive problems. Most cases of diarrhoea arise as a result of irritation of the bowel. This may be caused by a change of diet and even of water, by ingesting unsuitable material, by excitement, by an allergic response and by internal parasites. Homely remedies are often effective; these include the replacement of drinking water with an electrolyte and fluid replacement drink. Regular, small snacks of live yoghurt may also be useful. However, if the condition persists for more than a few days or if the dog's condition deteriorates the possibility that the condition is a symptom of something more serious should be considered and veterinary advice sought.

Dirofilaria immitis: *see* Heart worm

Distemper: *see* Canine distemper

Ear mites

Otodectes cynotis, a mite carried by both cats and dogs and capable of transferring from one to the other. Dogs with pendulous ears, which produce a warm damp environment much to the mite's liking, seem to be especially prone to infestation. This gives rise to canker (Otitis externa), which is characterized by dermatitis, inflammation, a waxy discharge and heat. It may be first noticed because the dog is scratching its ear and shaking its head. Antiparasitic eardrops will usually cure all but the most persistent infections. If damage has occurred to the ears, an Elizabethan collar may be used to prevent further harm and allow the existing damage to heal.

Eclampsia
Also known as milk fever and most commonly associated with lactating bitches.

Entropion
Inversion of the eyelids causing the lashes to rub against the eye itself. It may be the result of eye infection or be inherited. Breeds with heavily lidded eyes are most prone to the condition. Any puppy whose eyes are runny or sore should be treated with suspicion.

Epilepsy
Fits associated with abnormal brain function; may be induced by age, inherited, drugs and hormonal activity. Symptoms include collapse, convulsions, confusion, depression, ataxia, forced walking and dementia.

False pregnancy: *see*
Pseudopregnancy

Filaroides oslerii
A nematode that causes lesions in the trachea and bronchial linings giving rise to a dry cough.

Flatulence
A diet with inadequate fibre or consisting of stale food may give rise to flatulence. Changing the diet may resolve the problem.

Flea infestation
Infestation by *Ctenocephalides felis*:

I have just come from a swell
dog show he said I have
been lunching off a dog that was
worth at least one hundred/dollars a pound
> don marquis, *maxims of archy, archy and mehitabel* (1931)

Received wisdom tends to suggest that dogs and fleas are inseparable. It would not be at all difficult to fill this book with tales told over many years and in many ways to demonstrate the prevalence of the relationship. It would be facile to suggest that technology has solved the problem but it has made significant strides towards that end. The cat flea is the major source of flea infestation in dogs and may occasionally infest humans. *C. canis* confines its attentions to dogs and foxes. Any dog that shares its home with a cat or comes into contact with either wild or domesticated rabbits is likely, especially during the summer months, to provide a host for fleas. Some dogs appear to be indifferent to and unaffected by even a large population of fleas while others will scratch and lick incessantly even to the point of self-laceration. In both cases fleas are also the means by which a number of diseases are transmitted. Fleas spend most of their lives away from their host species awaiting the next opportunity to feed. Regular grooming is the best way of discovering the presence of fleas as well as of ridding the coat of the majority of fleas. If this routine is allied to vigorous use of the vacuum cleaner on carpets, rugs and furniture successful elimination may be achieved. The old adage that 'he who sleeps with dogs will rise with fleas' is no longer invariably applicable. The use of insecticidal spays, shampoos and impregnated collars should be regarded as a last resort rather than as a routine. Frequent use may develop resistant flea strains as well as allergic responses in the dog itself. A few unusually sensitive dogs or with poorly developed immune systems may develop allergy to the presence of fleas which manifests in the form of papules, hyperpigmentation, crusting of the skin and hair loss. Treatment is aimed at eliminating rather than repelling fleas coupled with topical treatment of the affected areas.

Fly strike

Coated dogs that are not regularly or properly groomed, particularly over the nether regions, may attract flies that will lay eggs and produce maggots. This tendency is sometimes offered as a reason for docking. It could equally well provide reason for less profuse coats and for better standards of care.

Fractures

Delicate breeds may fracture a limb by indulging in nothing more than unusually vigorous activity. More robust breeds may do so as the result of some form of trauma, a fight, a fall or a violent collision with some unyielding object.

Furunculosis

Anal furunculosis.

Gastric ulceration

Persistent blood-infused vomit, weight loss, a poor appetite and anaemia may all be causes by gastric ulcers that may be resolved by adjustments to the diet or may require veterinary treatment.

Gastritis

Vomiting either occasional or persistent; may be caused by eating unsuitable food, bacteria or viral infections or poisons and may be resolved by a change of diet.

Gingivitis: *see* Periodontal disease

Glossitis

Ulcerative glossitis.

Guardia

A parasite of the small intestine of dogs and several other mammals, including man. It can be present without producing discernible symptoms, but also may cause intermittent, sometimes blood-stained diarrhoea in which infective cysts are passed in large numbers. Prevention is difficult if dogs are exercised over land frequented by other, unprotected dogs. Attention to hygiene, especially of exercise runs and eating and drinking utensils, is important and should infection occur a period of quarantine would reduce the chance of reinfection. No treatment is currently licensed in Britain but routine treatment with fenbendazole is effective.

Haematuria

Produced by poisoning, kidney disease, viral infections and infection or trauma of the genital tract.

Harvest mites

Trombicula autumnalis; one of several species of acarine mites many of which readily transfer between a number species, including man, and which give rise to prurient dermatitis. Principally found in chalky rural areas at the end of dry summers. Washing with an antiparasitic shampoo will cure the condition and the avoiding of pasture during the late summer will prevent, reduce and may eliminate infestation. Some dogs appear to be exceptionally sensitive to infestation between the pads of their feet and will indulge in excessive and sometime self-damaging licking.

Heat stroke

In spite of extensive publicity every year, unthinking owners leave dogs in cars in which, even on a mildly warm day, can become so hot that its occupants are literally cooked alive. To an only slightly reduced effect, dogs confined in unshaded concrete runs or cages and dogs wearing an inappropriate form of muzzle also suffer. Dogs, especially the short faced brachycephalic breeds, those that are overweight, carry a heavy coat or are dark in colour or suffer from breathing or cardiac problems do not tolerate heat well. Dogs get rid of excessive heat by panting; they do not have the ability to do so by sweating, as does our own species. Once the ambient temperature begins to approach the dog's normal body temperature (106°F, 41°C) the dog will begin to show signs of distress. The onset of heat stroke is characterized by frantic, noisy panting, an expression of panic, a reddening of the tongue and mucous membranes and the drooling of viscous saliva. As the condition progresses, the dog may vomit, will emit blood-infused diarrhoea and stagger. The next stage results in coma and death. Emergency treatment must be carried out as quickly as possible if the dog's life is to be saved: take the dog to a cooler place, if a cool wet cloth can cover it, do so, immerse it in cool water for a few minutes and apply ice packs to its body. Unless the dog fully recovers very quickly it should be taken to a veterinary surgeon forthwith.

Heart worm

Dirofilaria immitis; symptoms of infection include hypersensitivity and dermatitis.

Hepatitis

Infectious canine hepatitis or jaundice gives rise to vomiting, pain, dehydration and yellowing of the mucous membranes. Preventive vaccination is better and more efficacious than treatment.

Hip dysplasia

A disease most often associated with large, heavy breeds in which the top of the femur is misshapen and the socket in the hip is shallow. Overweight puppies reared on hard ground or over-exercised may exaggerate the condition. Buyers should seek reassurance that the parents have been examined for the condition and should be suspicious of any puppy with an abnormal gait. A similar condition occurs in our own species.

Hookworm

Unicinaria stenocephala.

Uncinaria stencephala, a parasite that produces diarrhoea and eczema, mild blood loss and enteritis, particularly in groups or packs of dogs, especially when they are housed together and when they are exercised in well-used grass runs. Eggs are passed in the faeces and develop into larvae that are then ingested by dogs. Protect by avoiding the feeding of raw meat that is unsuitable for human consumption and ensure that dogs do not scavenge on carcases. Fenbendazole provides effective treatment.

Hypothermia

Adult dogs are far more tolerant of low temperatures than is our own species. Some breeds, not always those that originate in cold climates, will happily and comfortably curl up and snooze in snow. Foxes, which have similar physiological characteristics to small dogs, seek shelter underground or in a sheltered place above ground from very low temperatures, but they seldom seem to be harmed by their privations. Even so, dogs should be provided with comfortable, dry and secure beds whether in the house or in a kennel. If a dog falls into icy water but is still conscious when it is rescued it should be rubbed vigorously with dry towels both to remove the water and to stimulate circulation. If it will take a drink of warm liquid then so much the better.

Hyperkeratosis
Alopecia produced by hormone imbalance or distemper.

Incontinence, faecal
The inability to retain faecal material is often associated an injury to or malfunction of the anal sphincter.

Incontinence, urinary
It is important to distinguish between a dog that has not been properly house-trained or which wilfully chooses to soil in inappropriate places and one which, as a consequence of illness or old age, is genuinely incontinent. Puppies may pass urine if they are nervous or threatened. Older dogs may dribble it if they have cystitis, bladder stones, tumours or, in the case of males, an enlarged prostate gland.

Infectious canine hepatitis: *see* Hepatitis

Infectious canine tracheobronchitis: *see* Kennel cough

Infectious enteritis
Painful Inflammation of the intestine giving rise to diarrhoea and electrolyte imbalance. A number of causes may be implicated, including bacterial infection, viruses and ingestion of chemicals, adulterated food or parasitic infection.

Infectious haemoglobinuria: *see* Babesiosis

Interdigital cyst
May be caused by an accumulation of material on the hair between the toes or by the ingress of a foreign body. Keeping the hair well trimmed and frequent inspection, especially after exercise on hot days on tarmac surfaces, is the best preventive. If a cyst develops, excision by a vet may be necessary.

Intussusception
Severe enteritis that may be caused by distemper or worm infestation. Indicated by vomiting, diarrhoea, mucus-covered excrement and abdominal pain. Treat for worms and diarrhoea.

Kennel cough: *see* Canine adenovirus

Keratitis
A bacterial, viral or fungal infection, especially in brachycephalic dogs; indicated by copious production of tears, corneal dystrophy, blue eye or lens luxation. Treat with antibiotics.

Keratoconjunctivitis sicca
Dry eye resulting from conjunctivitis, foreign bodies in the eye or ulceration. Treat with antibiotics.

Ketosis
Stilted, unco-ordinated movement and vomiting. May indicate an advanced case of diabetes, malnutrition, poisoning and may

also be seen in lactating bitches. Veterinary diagnosis and treatment are required.

Lameness
May be caused by a wide range of conditions and, in the absence of obvious causes that will respond to home treatment, requires veterinary treatment.

Laryngitis
Bacterial or viral infection; the presence of foreign bodies should be considered.

Leishmaniasis
This is transmitted by sand flies and in Mediterranean countries is a common infection in dogs. Although the vectors do not yet occur in Britain (though global warming may alter this situation), warnings about the seriousness of allowing leishmaniasis to become established were being voiced well before 1990. Small colonies have been identified in the Channel Islands and a small rise in temperature could lead to its becoming established in southern England. Several forms of South American bacillae cause chronic skin infections. The European form gives rise to visceral disease that results in chronic debility, weight loss, enlargement of the liver and spleen and inflammation of the joints. The effect of treatment is problematical.

Lens luxation
A condition in which the lens becomes detached; may be caused by injury to the eye, but the tendency appears to be familial and is common in some terrier breeds.

Leptospirosis
Infection by *Leptospira iterrogans canicola*; Leptospirosis icterohaemorrhagiae is a bacteria-borne disease which gives rise to anaemia and jaundice, abortion and stillbirth. The disease is frequently fatal and is transmitted by infected rats and can produce serious human disease. Vaccination produces effective protection. Symptoms include loss of appetite, fever, blood-infused vomit, black diarrhoea, severe abdominal pain, reluctance to move and resentment at being handled, followed by collapse.

Lice infestation
Trichodectes canis bites and *Linognathus setosus* sucks; both types give rise to irritation, causing some dogs to rub, scratch and be restless although others seem to adopt a more philosophical attitude to the presence of a louse or two. Regular grooming will reveal infestations before they become extensive; they can be treated with appropriate insecticidal preparations. But heavy infestations of sucking lice, which are unlikely to occur in well-cared for dogs, may give rise to serious anaemia.

Lick granuloma
Often referred to as a 'hot spot' or 'wet eczema' and resulting from constant licking and caused by an irritant or boredom. The skin becomes thickened, red and sore. Investigate the reason for the licking and treat accordingly.

Liver disease: *see* Hepatitis

Lungworm
This is a group of parasites including *Filaroides*, *Oslerus* and *Angiostrongylus* species that invade respiratory and pulmonary tracts. Suitable anthelmintics provide effective treatment

Mange: *see* Demodectic and Sarcoptic mange

Misalliance
Veterinary and welfare campaigns to persuade owners to routinely have their dogs

neutered are based almost entirely on the desire to prevent the birth of unwanted puppies. A number of other less drastic means of contraception exist and these have been discussed elsewhere. If a fertile bitch contrives to get herself mated she should be taken to a veterinary surgeon within a day or two and will then receive a hormone injection that will terminate the pregnancy. She will not suffer the trauma endured when women undergo abortions and will quickly return to her customary state. However, she may redouble her efforts to get mated and should be kept closely confined during subsequent seasons as repeated treatment may have untoward side effects.

Mite infestation, ear mites, Otodectes

This causes irritation leading to head shaking, rubbing and scratching; this sometimes gives rise to secondary trauma in the inner ear. Mites are perhaps most often transmitted by cats. Treatment with a suitable preparation is simple and usually effective.

Narcolepsy

Dogs spend more time sleeping than do people. Puppies and older dogs spend more time asleep than do young and healthy adults and some spend far more time asleep than is normal. In the worst cases the animals suffer loss of voluntary muscular function and cataplexy especially associated with excitement produced by food, play or sexual activity. There is no cure and the condition may have an inherited element. Dogs suffering from narcolepsy should not be bred from. Dogs do not seem to suffer from insomnia.

Nasal discharge

Elderly dogs may produce a profuse nasal discharge, much the same as do some old people, other causes may may be rhinitis, a foreign body in the nose, sinusitis, a bronchial condition, distemper or poisoning. Treatment is dependent on the diagnosis.

Neosporosis Caninum

A parasite only rarely found in Britain that attacks the brain and nevous system leading, unless treated, to permanent damage or death within a few days. The parasite is found in fresh beef, even beef regarded as fit for human consumption. Freezing or cooking the meat will kill the parasites.

Nephritis

Renal failure arising out of any one of a number of causes. Veterinary diagnosis and treatment are indicated.

Ocular discharge

Most often found in brachycephalic breeds with large eyes and often associated with nasal or ocular foreign bodies, distemper, allergy or lead poisoning.

Obstructions

Plastic toys that can be chewed and swallowed but not digested should be avoided, as should rawhide toys and chews from unknown foreign sources that may not have eliminated every possibility of containing poisonous substances or exotic infections.

Otocariasis: *see* Ear mites

Otodectic mange, also called Demodicosis, follicular mange, red mange

Most dogs carry some *Demodex canis* mites which are kept under effective control by the immune system. If the population becomes excessive, cure is problematical and consists of frequent bathing with an insecticidal shampoo.

Parvovirus infection

The first veterinary response to the earliest

cases of parvovirus, which appeared in Britain in 1978, was that the condition was a product of the febrile imagination of breeders. Other animals suffered from a similar condition and it was subsequently suspected that one of the agent had mutated to enable it to attack dogs. Because they had no field immunity, many, particularly puppies and old dogs, died. There was no vaccine available that was licensed for use on dogs and many vets made illicit use of a vaccine licensed for cats. A dog-specific vaccine was subsequently developed and the disease has now been deprived of its most virulent effect. The disease is characterized by blood-infused, dark diarrhoea that emits a sweet, sickly smell. Infected puppies may be left with a damaged heart. The treatment of mild cases may rely on replacing solid food with electrolyte drinks or yoghurt, but any other than very mild cases should receive veterinary treatment.

Patella luxation

Most commonly associated with small breeds in which the kneecap becomes detached. May be the result of injury or an inherited condition. Affected dogs are characterized by lifting and hopping on one hind limb. This does not usually manifest in puppies but will certainly do so in their parents.

Poisons

Every home contains a pharmacopoeia of poisons ranging from the slightly toxic to the deadly, and, given the wide range of poisonous substances with which a dog may come into contact, it is surprising that so few dogs are actually poisoned. Treatment is likely to be effective if it is known what poison has been ingested, without this information treatment must rely on symptoms to indicate what might be most appropriate. A number of common houseplants may produce a rash, particularly around the mouth, after contact.

Others produce pain, swelling and soreness. Some are toxic to a degree that will induce vomiting, abdominal pain, cramps, tremors and heart, respiratory and kidney problems. Corrosive poisons include ammonia, oven cleaners, paint strippers, dishwashing powder and fluid, creosote and some strong disinfectants. Equally dangerous are slug baits, rodent poisons and weedkillers. Poisons may be categorized, albeit quite unscientifically, according to the treatment required to alleviate the symptoms: depending on the nature of the poison, acidic or alkaline, the dog should be made to vomit, using a small piece of washing soda, salt or mustard; for *acidic* poisons a small amount of bicarbonate of soda, or for *alkaline* poisons vinegar or lemon juice will help to ease the situation. The most common poisons listed by the Veterinary Poisons Information Service (VPIS) in-clude: ibuprofen, difenacoum, bromadiolone, paracetamol, metaldehyde, contraceptives, salbutamol, borax, poison from adder bites, chocolate, glyphosate, diclofenac, bone meal, paraquat, coumatetralyl, fertilizers, alphachloralose; to these should be added 4-D, cannabis, dyes, mecoprop, silica gel, terfenadine, chlorophacinone, nitrazepam, chlopyrifos, wallpaper paste and rodenticides. Commonly or occasionally encountered poisonous plants are belladonna, bluebell, blue-green algae, box, clematis, cut flower food, daffodils, fly agaric, fungi, garden bulbs, horse chestnut, hyacinth, hydrangea, ivy, laburnum, laurel spurge, lily-of-the-valley, lupin, mistletoe, oleander, rhododendron, sweetpea, wisteria.

Dogs that are allowed to wander at will, to scavenge or which have free access to parts of the house, especially garages and workshops, in which poisonous substances are stored are more likely to come into contact with poisons than are dogs that are better cared for and live in a well-ordered household. The possibility exists that the use of gas and poison rather than hounds to control foxes would result in an increase in the number of companion dogs that get access to carelessly placed poisons. In some of these cases it may not always be possible to identify the particular poison. In these cases diagnosis and treatment become problematical. Signs of discomfort, blistering around the mouth, panting, unusually nervous or lethargic behaviour, blisters around the lips, vomiting, a distinctive odour or the circumstantial evidence provided by the nearby use of toxic substances by gardeners, farmers and local authorities should all be used to provide information needed if treatment is to be most effective.

Dogs that have been poisoned should be kept quiet and warm and the respiration and pulse monitored. Home treatment for mild cases poses a choice between inducing vomiting or not doing so.

Induce vomiting: Antifreeze, ant-killer, arsenic, aspirin, atropine, barbiturates, barium, boric acid, plant bulbs, camphor, tobacco, codeine, cough syrups, DDT, digitalis, fly poisons, ink, iodine, iron tablets, lead, lighter fuel, metaldehyde, methalated spirit, mercury, mothballs, mushrooms and toadstools, nicotine, paint, phosphorus, plant sprays, thallium, santonin, shoe polish, weed killers, wintergreen oil. Vomiting may be induced by the administration of a finger nail-sized piece of washing soda or rock salt.

Do not induce vomiting: Acids, aconite, alkilis, ammonia, car polish, benzine, bleach, carbolic acid., carbon tetrachloride, cleaning fluid, kerosene, lye, paraffin, sulphuric acid. Seek urgent veterinary advice.

Pressure sores
Old dogs that are inclined to rest in the same position for prolonged periods may, as a consequence, develop pressure sores. These tend to occur towards the root of the tail or on the joints. Short of following an old dog around so that a soft cushion can be put in place should it decide to take a rest, the best method is to anoint any bare patches of skin with baby lotion. This will keep the skin soft and supple and so help to prevent sores.

Pseudopregnancy
Some bitches will mimic the symptoms of pregnancy after each season. They will grow rotund, produce milk, make beds and even go through a charade of whelping, after which they may adopt some live animal or inanimate object to serve as their offspring. Behavioural changes may include increased aggression, destructive behaviour, hyperactivity or lethargy and a grey vulval discharge. Pseudopregnancy among wild canids enables non-breeding females to help in rearing another bitch's young. To this extent it is not only a normal but also a useful process. However, the condition is inconvenient for owners and needs to be treated by a veterinary surgeon in order to suppress the symptoms. Spaying may also induce pseudopregnancy.

Pyometra
Bacterial infection of the uterus may occur during oestrus and develop when the cervix has closed at the end of the cycle. The bitch may initially seem to be no more than slightly off colour, go off her food and become unusually lethargic. The routine use of injections to postpone or subdue oestrus may increase the risk of pyometra. A study of almost 12,000 dogs (M. Niskanen, M. V. Thrusfield, 'Associations between age, parity, hormonal therapy and breed, and pyometra in Finnish dogs', *Vet. Rec.*, 31 October 1998) refuted the possibility by finding no correlation between the use of progestin and the incidence of pyometra, but a slight increase was associated with the use of

oestrogen. Bitches that had not been bred from had a slightly increased risk of developing pyometra compared with those that had had one or more litters. A discharge, often foul smelling, may be produced and at this stage veterinary assistance needs to be quickly sought. In some cases the uterus may be cleaned by the use of antibiotics, but in most surgical removal of the uterus is indicated. The seriousness and rapid onset of the condition is sometimes proposed as a reason for routine spaying but the potential side effects do not support the suggestion.

Prognathia

Protrusion of the lower jaw. The normal alignment of the jaws puts the teeth of the upper jaw slightly in front of those of the lower one, the mandible. In some brachycephalic breeds a protruding lower jaw and consequently protruding lower teeth are regarded as acceptable, but in most breeds it is anathema. If the milk teeth lie in front of those of the upper jaw the condition is likely to become more pronounced when the permanent teeth appear and as the mandible continues to grow. Unless the breed is one in which the conformation is acceptable, such puppies should be rejected and on no account should they ever be bred from.

Progressive retinal atrophy (PRA)

An inherited, degenerative disease of the retina initially giving rise to an inability to see in poor light and progressively to blindness.

Rabbit fur mite

Cheyletiella yasguri, sometimes referred to as 'walking dandruff' because of its microscopic size and slow movement. Infestation gives rise to mild dermatitis in dogs and to a stronger purity reaction in humans. Insecticidal shampoos for the infested dog and its contacts will eliminate the problem.

Rabies

Hydrophobia; certainly one of the most dreaded of all zoonoses. Transmitted by the bite of an infected animal and very occasionally by aerosol transmission. Once symptoms have appeared a fatal outcome is inevitable. The early Romans referred to rabies as *scorbutus*. Pliny, born in AD23, had much to say about rabies. He expressed the view that 'madness in dogs is dangerous to human beings when Sirius, the dog star, was shining' and so partially refuted Aristotle's confident denial that rabies posed a threat to man's well-being. Within the next 150 years both Siranus of Ephesus and Dioscorides were fully convinced not only that man could contract rabies but also that it could be contracted as the result of a bite from a mad dog. Informed opinion about rabies had changed dramatically.

The first reports of a disease with symptoms very similar to rabies date from about twenty-five centuries ago. The introduction of quarantine at the beginning of the twentieth century and kept Britain rabies-free for a hundred years, apart from infected dogs being brought into the country by soldiers returning from World War One. Every one of the few cases of rabies had been contracted overseas. The absolute requirement that every susceptible animal should undergo six months in quarantine was ended with the introduction of PETS. It was argued that the attendant documentation, examination of incoming animals and compulsory vaccination provided at least a similar degree of protection. It may seem unlikely that reliance on bureaucracy, inadequate surveillance and vaccines, which cannot ever be expected to be 100 per cent reliable, will prove as effective as quarantine has been. The first symptoms of the disease are innocuous and liable to be confused with the onset of some less serious condition – nervousness, a depraved appetite, unprovoked aggression, a high-pitched voice and a glazed expression. These symptoms may become more pronounced and develop into 'furious rabies' or may subside into 'dumb' rabies, in which the animal seems almost stupefied. There is no effective treatment and all infected animals face a lingering and horrific death.

Rickettsias

These are a series of bacterial infections of which *Rhipicephalus sanguineus* is the principal vector. Infection gives rise to Boutonneuse fever. Transmission is via fleas and ticks, either direct or from rodents.

Ringworm

Microsporum canis; not a worm at all but a fungus that attacks the outer layers of the skin and hair fibres, resulting in the characteristic circular patch of bare skin. The fungi can be picked up from contaminated soil or surfaces as well as from other animals. It is unsightly but superficial and easily eliminated.

Roundworm

Toxacara canis.

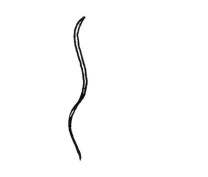

Toxacara cati.

Toxacariasis and toxocariasis are diseases sometimes transmitted to humans as a consequence of infestation with *Toxascaris leonine*, a parasite found in dogs, cats fox and a number of wild carnivores, and *Toxocara canis*, found in dogs and foxes. *Toxocara cati*, found in cats, should also be implicated but is seldom mentioned as a possible culprit. In fact, the incidence of human infection even among those who may have antibodies to the parasite is very low (O. Barriga, 'A critical look at the importance, prevalence and control of toxocariasis and the possibility of immunological control', *Vet. Parasitology*, vol. 29, pp. 195–223). Roundworm is not a parasite exclusively found in dogs, thus to place entire blame for the presence of the diseases on dogs and to exaggerate its importance is hugely unjust. For some years the received wisdom has been that roundworm infection is transmitted through contact soil laden with eggs or larvae. This ignored the fact that cats, foxes and other creatures that may carry roundworm infestations may also have contaminated the soil. Indeed, it would not have been unreasonable to suggest that, when places to which dogs did not have access were found to be contaminated, some other culprit should be regarded as the prime suspect. This simple logic did not appeal to those who regarded *Toxocara* as something to be used in order to promote dislike of dogs and their owners. They were adamant that people, especially children, were at risk of being blinded as a consequence of contact with contaminated soil. In fact, though rare instances of eye damage have been recorded, none appear to have resulted in blindness and none have proved that the source of the infection was dogs. All of which became largely academic in 2003 when A. Wolfe and I.P. Wright ('Human toxocariasis and direct contact with dogs', *Vet Rec.*, 5 April 2003) showed that dogs' coats may harbour fertile eggs and that these might be ingested by people who came into direct contact with these dogs. The authors concluded that, 'the evidence already in the literature provides strong evidence for a link between direct contact with dogs and toxocariasis. ... The authors consider that direct contact with dogs may play a more important role than soil contamination in the epidemiology of human toxocariasis.' The conclusions were at once both alarming and comforting: alarming in that they demonstrated that human toxocariasis might derive from contact with dogs whose coats contained fertile *Toxocara* eggs, and comforting in that regular worming, frequent grooming and strict attention to hygiene should eliminate almost of the risk. Good breeders often worm all their dogs regularly, they worm pregnant bitches and puppies from the age of two weeks, and by the time they are ready to go to their new homes they should be virtually free of infestation. Routine worming thereafter should maintain this situation. Fenbendazole provides the best treatment currently available. Apart from the fact that the drug is effective against a range of internal parasites, its efficacy is increased by a routine that spreads the dosage over several days. It comes in a variety of forms – paste, liquid, granules and most recently attractive titbits. It is also one of the cheapest worming preparations available and is obtainable direct from chemists selling veterinary preparations and agricultural merchants.

Rubarth's disease: *see* **Infectious canine hepatitis**

Stings
Dogs often react with something that seems close to panic to bee or wasp stings, and by biting at the area may harm themselves. Bee stings should be scraped from the skin, not pulled out, which tends to inject more venom into the wound. No further treatment other than keeping the dog calm until the pain has subsided is necessary. Wasps do not leave their stings in their victims and are capable of inflicting several stings. These, because wasps may feed on carrion, can easily become infected and should be thoroughly cleansed and treated with a disinfectant. Stings around and in the mouth that may cause swelling that interferes with breathing should be watched carefully.

Tapeworm
Taenia, a genus of large tapeworms of which *Taenia brauni*, *T. hydatigena*, *T. krabbei*, *T. multiceps*, *T. ovis*, *T. pisiform* and *T. seralis* may infect dogs as well as a number of wild carnivores, rodents, ruminants, rabbits and hares. Some species also infect man, causing large hydatid cysts that pose an appreciable health risk. Similar cysts also occur in sheep and reduce the value of carcases. Major sheep-rearing countries, although not Britain, often impose stringent controls in order to protect the value of carcases. Effective control is

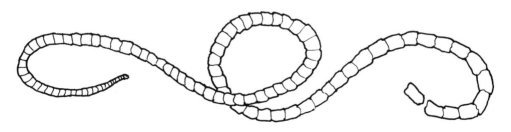

Taenia avis.

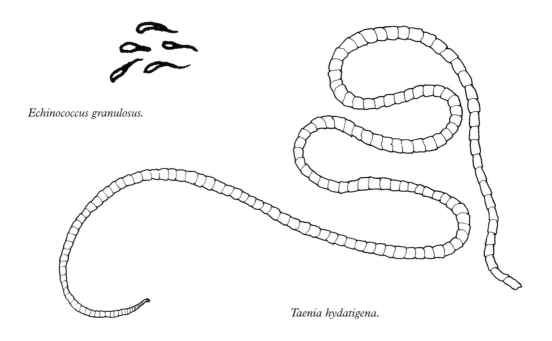

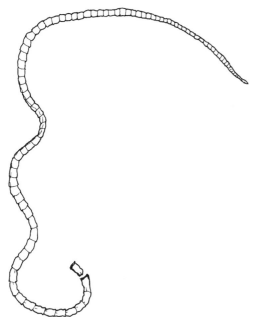

Echinococcus granulosus.

Taenia hydatigena.

Taenia pisiformis.

available by means of routine dosing with fenbendazole. *Echinococcus granulosus* a small tapeworm found in dogs, foxes and cats that can infect humans causing dangerous hydatid cysts in the liver, lungs, kidneys and other organs. *Echinococcus multilocularis* is a parasite of dogs, with rodents as an intermediate host. It is widely distributed throughout the northern hemisphere and from the 1970s until the early 1990s increased in German foxes from 12.5 to 58.5 per cent. It is absent from Britain. This is a very serious disease of humans, has an incubation period of up to ten years and there is no satisfactory treatment.

Teeth

Most puppies are born without teeth, which erupt during the next three or four weeks to produce twenty-eight deciduous teeth, lacking only molars. Exceptionally strong deciduous teeth may be retained after the permanent teeth have begun to erupt. If left in place, the deciduous teeth may cause the permanent ones to take up a distorted formation that would be subject to exceptional wear during the rest of the dog's life. Malocclusions are an inherited condition that in the most severe cases are apparent in the position of the milk teeth but are more likely to become apparent when the permanent teeth erupt. Malocclusions lead to excessive wear on the teeth, to an untypical appearance and to the loss of any chance of success in the show ring. Because the tendency is inherited, dogs that exhibit them should not be bred from.

The retention of milk teeth will, if not treated, often lead to the permanent teeth being pushed out of line, sometimes referred to as a 'crowded mouth'. though this term may also be applied to irregular dentition arising out of large teeth in a short or narrow jaw. An overshot or brachygnathic bite is one in which the upper teeth project significantly beyond the lower teeth. A slight projection in which the teeth still meet is often referred to as a scissor bite and should be regarded as normal and desirable in the majority of breeds. An undershot or prognathic bite involves the lower teeth projecting beyond those of the upper jaw and is acceptable in very few brachycephalic breeds. A level bite in which the teeth tips of the upper and lower jaws meet should be regarded as a mild form of prognathism. It gives rise to rapid and excessive wear. Mild forms of these conditions may be the product of misplaced teeth but more severe forms are more often the result of abnormal growth or abnormal formation of the jaws. Each jaw consists of two major bones that normally grow in unison but if their growth is unsynchronized a wry, twisted jaw may be created Puppies and their parents should be examined to ensure that dentition is correct for the particular breed and no assurances from the breeder that a malocclusion will 'come right' should be entertained.

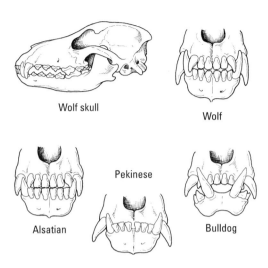

Types of mouth and dentition.

Some unethical breeders may resort to the use of homemade braces as a means to force the teeth into a normal occlusion. The long-term effect is to loosen the teeth and shorten their life. Loose teeth may be retained in their sockets and provide places that are likely to harbour gum infection, gingivitis, loosen more teeth and cause pain and bad breath. The first step towards a trouble-free mouth is normal dentition and jaw formation. The second is to provide the dog with dry food as part of its diet and to give it something to chew (a large uncooked bone is ideal) in order to cleanse its teeth and prevent gum disease and the accumulation of tartar. In recent years the regular use of toothpaste and toothbrush has become as much a matter of routine to maintain oral hygene and health in dogs as it is in people. Inspection of the teeth during each major grooming session will reveal the presence of any developing problems that require veterinary attention. Chipped, broken or loose teeth can quickly become infected and give rise to considerable pain. To inspect the teeth requires a degree of co-operation from the dog, allied with a degree of skill from the examiner. Even experienced breeders, owners and judges often unthinkingly cover the dog's eyes and are then surprised when it fails to co-operate. If the teeth are examined by using the thumbs to lift the gums to uncover the teeth, it is more likely to co-operate and so enable a thorough examination to be made.

Ticks

Ixodes sp.; within a matter of months after the introduction of PETS a number of exotic ticks began to be found in Britain. Some of these have serious health implications for both dogs and humans, and, unless control and surveillance are quickly and dramatically improved, will place an increased load on veterinary skills and NHS resources. The genus *Ixodes* comprises a number of species that may infest dogs; *I. angustus* is confined to dogs; *I. canisuga* is also found on foxes and other species; *I. cookie* is found on most species; *I. cornuatus* is found on dogs and other species and *I. hexagonus* is most commonly found on hedgehogs but may also infest dogs and other species. *Babesia canis* transmits babesiosis, also known as tick fever, Texas fever and redwater fever; it is a genus of protozoa transmitted by ticks and found in several species of animal, including dogs and man. Symptoms include anaemia, jaundice and blood-charged urine; its introduction to Britain may be the result of poor surveillance of animals imported under PETS.

Toxocariasis

Roundworm infestation.

Umbilical hernia

A soft swelling of the umbilicus to which some breeds appear to be particularly prone. The Kennel Club inexplicably insists that surgical repair interferes with the dog's normal conformation and thus allows dogs with hernias to be shown, but bans those in which the condition has been treated. A number of these conditions are to be found in our own species and others, as well as in several breeds of dog. Others appear to be confined to individual breeds about which honest breeders will be open and honest.

Urinary incontinence

Urinary incontinence may arise as part of the aging process or as a side-effect of spaying. Veterinary treatment is required.

Urticaria

Also called hives, this is characterized by localized swelling , which may itch and give rise to scratching. The cause may be allergic.

Whipworm

Trichuris vulpis.

Trichuris vulpis; a worm that infects the intestines and found in overused grass runs, in which eggs may remain viable for up to five years. Infestation is characterized by a persistent, dry cough but often no symptoms are apparent.

Wounds

The treatment of wounds is dependent on the amount of damage caused and their nature. The most important point is to ensure that the wound is clean. A clean, incised cut may be easily cleaned with warm water and a mild antiseptic. To dress the wound may need the protection afforded by an Elizabethan collar, if the dog is to be prevented from interfering with the dressing or the wound itself. A deep or large incision may require veterinary attention, and, if bleeding is profuse, a tight bandage or tourniquet may be required to staunch the flow of blood until professional treatment is available. Lacerations and contusions involve tears to the skin and underlying flesh; cleanliness is the first and unavoidable requirement, followed by a dressing, and, if necessary, the use of an Elizabethan collar to protect the dressing. Puncture and fistulous wounds, such as are caused by a penetrating bite, may have only a small but deep penetration that is not easily cleansed. If it is possible to do so and ensure that no foreign material remains in the wound, no further treatment may be necessary. It is, however, a wise precaution to consult a vet in order that an antibiotic injection may be considered as a means to avoid infection. Some owners of sporting dogs that may in the course of their work sustain injuries carry a small container of antiseptic with them. It seems a wise precaution.

Bites

Dogs may be bitten by other dogs or by anyone of several other domestic or wild animals. Whatever the cause, the bite needs to be thoroughly cleansed. Puncture wounds in particular need to be properly treated in case infection has been introduced deep into the cavity.

Burns

Burns may be caused by heat, caustic chemicals, excessive dry heat, excessive cold, electric shock and exposure to sunshine. It should be remembered that dogs with very short, dark coats are more likely to become sunburnt than are more profusely coated, light-coloured dogs. In severe cases antibiotics may be necessary.

Nose

The dog's nose conveys information to the dog in a way that is completely beyond our capabilities and even our imagination. Watch a dog in the Cruft's obedience competition go out into a carpeted area on which during the previous few days hundreds of dog and their handlers have trod and select just one small piece of paper from several identical ones simply on the basis that the paper carries the scent of its owner and you do no more than scratch the surface of the information conveyed by the dog's nose. It performs all the functions of any mammalian nose and is subjected to a similar range of problems. Snow-nose produces a lightening of a normally black nose to a brown or flesh colour; the condition tends to occur in winter and to disappear in summer, it is not harmful and no certain cure exists. Vitaligo has a similar, though usually less extreme effect and is associated with age rather than light, the condition may disappear spontaneously but no certain cure is known. Nasal callus produces a thickened and roughened skin and may be associated with distemper.

Obstructions

All dogs, and puppies in particular, much in the same way as babies, use their mouths to explore the characteristics of foreign objects. This may lead to their swallowing or attempting to swallow indigestible or poisonous material. The most common causes of problems are plastics, cooked bones, metal objects, twigs, nylon clothing and wrappings, and small stones, but the range of foreign objects that vets may be called upon to remove from a dog's alimentary tract almost beggars belief.

Skin

Once it is appreciated that every part of the external surface of a dog is covered with skin and that this surface is continually exposed to trauma, infection and the attentions of unwanted visitors, it will ready be understood why the skin tends to give rise to more problems than any other part of the body. Fortunately, the majority of these are easily resolved if they are caught early and treated appropriately.

Cruelty

It may not be difficult for an individual to arrive at a working definition of what he or she regards as cruelty, and from that point to leap to the conclusion that it would be equally easy to arrive a corporate definition that could be supported by the force of law. In fact, politicians, welfare agencies and even the veterinary profession have demonstrated an inability to produce a logically coherent definition of what should be regarded as cruelty. What is regarded as cruelty changes from place to place and from time to time.

There can be few practising Christians who would now approve of the appalling treatment supposedly meted out to the Gadarene swine, and certainly few countries in which such treatment would not incur the wrath of the law, but we have had the persecution of magpies for not wearing full mourning after the crucifixion and the association between Shrove Tuesday and organized cockfighting and bull baiting. Christianity is riddled with iconography that bears witness to ritualized cruelty.

It has been shown that there are parallels between animal abuse and child abuse and domestic violence. In Britain the response to this has been to seek means by which incidents are made known to all the agencies involved. In 2003 the Royal College of Veterinary Surgeons relaxed its *Guide to Professional Conduct* so that information about non-accidental injuries to dogs could be transmitted to the appropriate authorities.

For its part, the Kennel Club had long followed a policy of disciplining any owner or handler who subjects a dog taking part in any authorized activity to harsh treatment. The owner is likely to be banned from any further involvement in such activities either for a period of time or for life. Anyone convicted of cruelty to any animal would be subject to precisely the same treatment. The five freedoms described in Chapter 4 probably get closer than anything else to define the conditions in which cruelty does not occur.

Annual statistics published by the RSPCA demonstrate that cruelty, as defined in law, remains a problem within British society. Conversely, these same statistics also demonstrate that the existence of the RSPCA does not prevent cruelty. The second symposium sponsored by the RSPCA in 1976 on the mutilation of animals identified castration, spaying, tattooing, declawing, devoicing, ear-cropping, tail-nicking, docking, teeth-cutting and ear implants as morally unacceptable mutilations. Yet almost all of these are practised without being tested in the courts and without discernible objection by welfare organizations. Some of these mutilations enjoy the support of and sponsorship by these organizations.

Of the prosecutions successfully pursued by the RSPCA by far the greatest number involved neglect or abandonment. No studies appear to have been published that seek to discover whether there is any significant bias within the number of neglected or abandoned dogs towards any particular source of acquisition. It is possible that dogs acquired easily from puppy supermarkets rather than a breeder are in the majority; the latter is likely to need satisfying that the puppies will have a good home and to be available to provide advice and assistance. The representation of some pedigree breeds may also be reduced by the existence of breed-specific welfare and rescue schemes. These are intended to find homes for dogs that, for no reason of theirs, may have fallen on hard times: the owners may have died or become unable to provide continued care. Some schemes have homes waiting for dogs in need, but sadly some major welfare bodies are reluctant to co-operate with breed rescue, preferring, it seems, to destroy healthy dogs rather than hand them over to a breed rescue scheme that has a good and reliable home waiting for them.

10   Controls

Controls may be conveniently divided into two types: those imposed by national and local government and those imposed by the dog owners themselves. Licensing, preferably compulsory, is the measure most likely to be paraded as a panacea for all the problems for which dogs are blamed. The history of these controls is a shameful one that reflects no credit on those in power.

Licensing

The official imposition of a charge, whether it is referred to as a licence or as a tax, on dog ownership is not new. From King Cnut onwards officially imposed control measures have failed. Paragraph 31 of the

> *Carta de Foresta*, of King Canutus a Dane, and a King of this realme, graunted at a Parliament holden at Winchester, in the yeare of our Lord 1016 further decreed that 'no meane person, may keepe any Greyhounds: but freemen may keep Greyhounds, so that their knees be cut before the Verderors of the Forest and without cutting of their knees also, if they doe abide ten miles from the bounds of the Forest. But if they doe come any nearer to the Forest, they shall pay twelue pence for euery mile: but if the Greyhounds bee found within the Forest, the master or owner of the Dog shall forfeit the Dog, and ten shillings to the King.'

In addition, all mastiffs kept in the pro-scribed area were required to be expedited according to the laws of the forest. Expediting was carried out by placing a fore-foot 'on a piece of wood eight inches thick and a foot square, and then setting a chisel of two inches broad upon the three claws, he stuck them off with one blow of a mallet.' The operation was carried out on both fore-feet. 'If any Mastiff was found on any wild animal and he was mutilated, he whose dog he was quit of the deed; but if he was not mutilated, the owner of the mastiff was guilty as if he had given it with his own hand.' In addition, small dogs 'because it stands to reason there is no danger in them', could be kept without the need for mutilation. A small dog was defined as one that could be passed through a metal hoop of about 7in in diameter.

Surgical mutilation in various forms continued to be used as a means of controlling dogs and even reappeared in the 1980s in the form of a campaign supported by welfare organizations and the veterinary profession to require that dogs should be surgically neutered.

However, the major thrust of those who regard the control of dog ownership as a desirable end has largely been to argue the case for levying a tax on dogs or making licensing compulsory. In 1791 George Clark addressed Parliament on the subject of a tax upon dogs as a means to raise funds for 'effectually suppressing the oppressive practice of impressing seamen and more expeditions by manning the Royal Navy'. Clark believed that more dogs were kept 'for fancy or for pleasure, than from necessity', and that, since they could be regarded as luxuries, they should be taxed. Since he suggested that the collectors of the window tax should also collect this new tax, we might also conclude that he regarded windows as luxuries.

However, Clark was more honest than some of his successors and accepted that the tax 'would no doubt cause a devastation among those creatures' and even considered the possibility that 'laying the tax upon dogs will cause so many to be destroyed that the tax will be unproductive'. He therefore set out to 'enumerate some of the dangers and evils which arise from dogs' and so justify his proposal other than as a means to raise revenue to improve conditions in the Navy. Foremost among these were the fear of rabies, followed by the unnecessary consumption of food by dogs, the prevalence of poaching and harassment to farm livestock. Clark's proposals enjoyed the support of a small but vociferous minority, but it was

perhaps largely the prospect of raising an estimated £150,000 by means of the dog tax which most attracted Parliament and led to several debates during the next five years. The anticipated annual income assumed that half of the one million households in Britain contained one dog, yielding £125,000, and taxation on the estimated 5,000 gentlemen who kept packs for hunting would yield another £25,000. The tax was entirely ineffectual, the press gang continued to operate and thousand of dogs were killed or abandoned when the due date came round each year.

In the United Kingdom, with no dog licensing, the number of strays was estimated at 6.8 per cent of the total dog population; in the European countries in which licensing was compulsory the population of strays amounted to 11.2 per cent of the population. The evidence shows that compulsory licensing is either ineffective or actually increases the number of strays. It has since been claimed that the campaign to persuade owners to have their dogs neutered has

---

Strays

A survey carried out in 1990 by the European Parliament's Environment and Public Health Committee showed that:

Country	No. of dogs (M)	No. of strays (M)	Registration	Population (M)
Belgium	1.2	n.a.	voluntary	9.86
Denmark	0.45	no problem	compulsory	5.12
France	9.5	0.3	compulsory	55.62
Greece	0.53	0.15	compulsory	9.93
Ireland	0.6	0.15	compulsory	3.54
Italy	5.4	0.85	compulsory	57.29
Luxembourg	0.12	n.a.	none	0.37
Netherlands	1.2	n.a.	compulsory	14.62
Portugal	1.3	0.5	compulsory	10.29
Spain	3.0	n.a.	compulsory	38.89
West Germany	3.6	n.a.	compulsory	56.12
UK	7.3	0.5	none	61.1

Note: figures for Germany relate to the period before reunification

further reduced the number of strays in the United Kingdom.

We live in an age when we are bombarded with advertisements that seek to persuade us that various diets, exercise regimes, pills and potions will have us healthier, more attractive and restore youthful vigour. The greatest effect of the majority of these regimes is to make their purveyors richer and dog owners considerably poorer. Dog ownership has long been regarded as something that should be controlled by means of taxation as well as by more punitive means.

From 1796 until 1867, dog ownership was subjected to an assessed tax, the amount of which varied from time to time and according to the type of dog. In Britain the Customs and Inland Revenue Act of 1878 set the annual licence fee at 7s.6d (37½p). It remained at this figure until the government, having realized that it was costing £3.5 million to collect £750,000 in fees. In 1986 the government decided to abolish dog licensing, whereas the VAT levied on dog food yielded almost £1,500 million a year. In every country in which registration and licensing are compulsory the population of strays and abandoned dogs is far higher than in the United Kingdom. The fact that licensing had no discernible beneficial effect either in Britain or elsewhere did not seem to be taken into account. The alternative would have been to increase the licence fee to an economic level and to make licensing and the permanent identification of all dogs compulsory. This would inevitably have led to the slaughter of thousands of dogs and to many thousands more being abandoned.

In 2003, one misguided local authority proposed to regard anyone who owned more than six dogs as running a business. This would have required planning permission, the levy of business rates and invoked health and safety legislation. Better sense eventually prevailed, but the proposal was never the less symptomatic of the attitude of some myopic local authorities.

It is highly likely that the campaign has been a major contributory factor in the decline of the popularity of dogs as companions and the increased popularity of cats which are not subject to any such proposals, for which their owners are not legally responsible and which make fewer demands on their owners. Dog owners should escape the attentions of salesmen selling quack remedies that will ease the problems that may be associated with dog ownership. What follows eschews such quackery and concentrates on common sense and proven fact. It relies on the belief that every caring dog owner will want to exercise such control over his or her dog as will prevent it from being a nuisance to others, will protect its welfare and will make it more fun to own.

The law relating to the ownership and control of dogs has grown up piecemeal over many years and is now in something of a mess. The government has expressed the intention of producing an all-embracing Animal Welfare Act as a means to tidy the present situation and revising the law relating to dogs and their owners in order to make it more effective, to identify responsible agencies and to provide better standards of protection for dogs. This at least is what the government claims, but it would not be at all surprising if the opportunity were taken to respond to the vigorous welfare lobbies and introduce punitive controls that will make it more difficult and more expensive for people to enjoy the benefits of dog ownership. Governments of all persuasions appear to regard dogs as sources of nuisance and seem little aware of the benefits, social and economic, deriving from ownership.

Thefts

The existence of an extensive market for

stolen dogs, especially small pedigree breeds but also including the dogs that people involved in illicit and often brutal sports use, is not new, but in recent years appears to have become well organized. Stolen dogs are often not high among the crimes that come to the notice of the police. The owners themselves provide the most effective protection against thefts as well as the means to recover stolen dogs.

For just as long as dogs have been valued for the service, enjoyment, security, status and companionship they offer, so they have been attractive to thieves and other miscreants. There is nothing new about what appears to be a resurgence of dog thefts. Dogs are stolen because they have a resale value, either to their legitimate owners or to people who are prepared to ask no questions when they acquire a dog. The fortunate ones go to good homes, perhaps even better homes than they were stolen from. The unfortunate ones, depending on their type, may be used for any one of several nefarious purposes – baiting, fighting and transporting drugs, or, after being comprehensively brutalized, as guard dogs. Their lives are invariable miserable and short. What is new is that this is taking place in spite of the availability of sophisticated means of identification: tattoos, microchips, DNA sampling and other means are all available by which dogs can be positively identified. Yet, with the exception of DNA profiling, none are infallible and not all dogs are positively identified. During their early days microchips were treated with some suspicion. The very idea of inserting a foreign object into a dog was anathema to some owners, but fears have been reduced as more and more surgical procedures carried out on people make use of mechanical insertions. There were also fears that microchips would migrate or cease to function. These may have been justified for a while but improvements have taken place that makes

them groundless. National rescue agencies claim to ensure that every dog they rehome carries a microchip. This is not always supported by what happens in practice. In any case, many breed-specific rescue agencies make no attempt to identify permanently the dogs they place in new homes. Most national and some breed rescue agencies require that their clients undertake to return their dogs if circumstances make it impossible to keep them. Seldom are these agreements supported by the weight of the law. Even when they are legally binding, they are seldom enforced. If all rescue agencies were to co-operate it would be possible to provide rescued dogs with far better legal protection than they presently enjoy. Anyone who acquires a dog from a rescue or welfare kennel should verify whether or not it has been microchipped and should ensure that the chip is scanned to ensure that he or she is not about to acquire a stolen or lost dog. It is far better to clarify the situation before accepting the responsibilities of ownership than having, at a future date, to face a dispute in the courts about ownership.

The ease with which registration and other documents can be fraudulently obtained makes it possible to enhance the sale price of stolen dogs. Perhaps worse still, stolen dogs can be bred from and their offspring readily accepted for registration. By such means is the worth of the Kennel Club's registration system devalued and those who purchase registered puppies are comprehensively defrauded. There is little evidence that suggests that the Club is at all concerned to make its registration system less readily available to thieves and fraudsters.

At the end of 2003 the Kennel Club launched an extension to its existing services that linked microchips with mobile phones. To what extent this will deter thieves or lead to their capture remains to be seen, but the new service certainly represents a

considerable step forward in enabling owners as well as rescue agencies to trace dogs
that have strayed or been taken from their
homes. The new service goes a long way
towards making other systems, whether
based on the microchip or not, obsolete. It
also makes it unnecessary for dogs to be
compulsorily identified. Compulsory, permanent identification would make life less
easy for thieves and fraudsters and would go
some way towards protecting dogs from
their attentions. Fraudulent registrations
and fraud at shows and other competitions
would be reduced. The only possible objection might stem from the cost involved, but,
if owners value their dogs, some cost is
inevitable. The unpalatable fact is that dog
thieves individually and nationally seem to
have been better organized than owners, rescue agencies, the police and the Kennel
Club. They thrive because attempts to bring
them to book tend to be half-hearted at best
and misdirected at worst. However, technology is now available which will enable owners to trace strayed and stolen dogs.

Apart from any intrinsic value they may
possess, dogs are valued as an integral part
of the family. This makes them attractive targets for thieves. There is nothing new about
the dishonourable profession of dog thieving
– it has been going on ever since the affinity
between dog and man was established, it
even has its place in the writings of such
authors as Jaraslov Hasek and Virginia
Woolf. What is new is that, as the means to
protect dogs from being stolen become more
readily available and more sophisticated, the
number of dogs stolen seems to be increasing. They may be stolen for resale or in order
that a ransom can be demanded from their
legitimate owners, a few may be kept for
breeding. These are the fortunate ones, we
have noted what happens to the less fortunate. A growing number are slaughtered and
their skins used to make fashion accessories

*A gate can be used to confine a dog to part of
the house or to keep two dogs apart.*

and garments. Sadly, few police authorities
seem to take the problem seriously although
there is evidence that attitudes are beginning
to change. Even welfare societies seem not to
have the problem high on their agendas.
Owners must do what they can as individuals and collectively.

Thieves who have made off with a haul of
valuable breeding stock and puppies have
targeted a number of breeders. Their loss
may be greater, but is not felt more deeply
than when a family loses a much loved companion. Breeders are aware of the problem
and the most of the far-sighted co-operate
with their fellows in order to make life less
easy for thieves. The owners of companion
dogs may not be aware that a problem exists,
let alone of its extent. However, they can
take a few simple steps that will provide their
pets with a far greater degree of protection:

• Never buy a puppy unless you can see its
  mother, it might have been stolen.

- Never buy a puppy other than from a reputable breeder.
- Never disclose your dog's pet name to strangers.
- Sensible owners no longer plaster their cars with advertising stickers which provide information that thieves might regard as an invitation.
- Ensure that you have photographic records of all your dogs and puppies.
- Do not leave transport cages or grilles in a car when they are not in use.
- Never leave dogs unattended in the garden, at public events or in the car.
- Never allow your dog to run out of sight when at exercise, especially in a public park.
- Always ensure that runs and the kennel are secure: a stout lock, a dense and thorny hedge or a strand of barbed wire can be used to make it difficult to reach into a fenced run.
- Install a reliable alarm system: those intended for garages are cheap, easily installed and can be effective deterrents.
- Do not advertise your address or allow anyone else, including canine societies, breed clubs or local newspapers to do so.
- If you suspect that your premises are attracting attention from possible thieves, make a note of the number and type of car and write a description of occupants; pass your suspicions and information on to the police and to other local owners.
- Treat any unexpected callers with suspicion; it is best not to allow them on the premises, but, if you allow them to see puppies, take a photograph on the pretext that it will be a memento for them.
- Should you lose any dogs to thieves do not place great faith in rewards, these do little other than encourage thefts.
- Do not place great faith in any means of so-called permanent identification, by far the best method currently available relies

on a microchip implanted under a dog's skin but all can be easily removed; DNA profiling is obviously safe from this.
- Insurance will not prevent a dog from being stolen, but it might provide the resources needed to mount a search; the law currently insists that dogs should, at all times, wear a collar with a metal tag which gives information that will allow the animal to be identified; the metal tag also provides all the information needed by a thief to attempt to extract a ransom from the rightful owner.
- If your dog is stolen inform the police, local rescue and welfare kennels, local vets, the breeder, local canine societies and appropriate breed clubs.
- Some local newspapers as well as the weekly canine press will publish details of stolen dogs that may make them less easy to sell.

The prime objective is to protect your dog from thieves. Young pedigree dogs have a considerable resale value, older ones may be ransomed, bitches can be used to produce a litter before being discarded, sporting breeds may become involved in illegal activities and a number of breeds may be used to provide material for the fashion industry. Owners who have a genuine care for their dogs will do their utmost to deter thieves but they should never lose sight of the fact that potential thieves are endlessly devious.

Neutering

Welfare agencies and the veterinary profession advocate neutering as a means to prevent the birth of unwanted puppies and claim that their campaign is having a significant effect. In 2001 a survey carried out by the Association of British Dogs and Cats Homes (ABDCH) reported that over 96,000 dogs had been rescued and 65,000 had been rehomed. The survey did not report on how many of these had been neutered. In the USA it has been suggested that a high divorce rate contributes to the number of dogs being placed in rescue kennels (Dr Jack Britt at the BVA Congress, Exeter, 1985). It is, of course, true that neutered dogs do not produce unwanted puppies, but neither do well cared for dogs owned by responsible owners.

Too often neutering is promoted as a panacea for behavioural problems on which it has little or no effect. Neutering offers some benefits to the dog, but it may also produce undesirable side effects. Proper care is far more preferable than surgery as a means to prevent the birth of unwanted puppies. It is not part of the purpose of this book to enable feckless owners to avoid the consequences of poor standards of care, it is intended to encourage proper standards. But if, as they sometimes will, accidents occur, the means to prevent the birth of puppies exist and are far less traumatic and far less expensive than surgery.

Castration and Spaying

Castration and spaying (ovariohysterectomy) are the two forms of surgical neutering most energetically promoted both by welfare agencies and by the veterinary profession. Both are more invasive and, therefore, more traumatic than other forms of surgical neutering. They are also the most likely to give rise to subsequent unwanted side effects. Other forms of surgical neutering include vasectomy in dogs and tubal ligation in bitches.

The spaying of bitches is sometimes necessary as a form of treatment for any one of a number of uterine infections. Spaying is also vigorously promoted as a means of preventing bitches from having unwanted puppies. Spayed bitches tend to have a reduced incidence of mammary tumours, but also may develop side effects that cannot be said to be health promoting, and castrating dogs, particularly cryptorchids (*see* below), is an equally certain way of preventing testicular tumours.

The most obvious drawback is that all surgery is accompanied by some degree of risk. As regards neutering, the risks are small but should not be dismissed. Nor should the likelihood that castrated dogs and spayed bitches may develop characteristics that do not reflect what they owner regards as desirable. Neutering may cause some dogs to grow heavy or woolly coats that are not characteristic of the breed. It may, particularly in bitches, increase aggression. Castrated dogs may also become sexually attractive to other dogs. There is also debate about why neutered dogs have a tendency to become obese. One view suggests that, because neutered dogs tend to be more lethargic, they also tend to put on weight. Others suggest that a survey that examined the effect of castration on behaviour (R.J. Maarschalkerweerd *et al.*, 'Influence of orchiectomy on canine behaviour', *Vet Rec.*, 14 June 1997) found that inappropriate sexual behaviour towards people, male and male dogs roaming in search of bitches in season, aggression, abnormal urination in the home were markedly reduced.

Studies (for instance, by A.R. Michell, 'Neutering and longevity in dogs', *Vet Rec.*, 14 March 1998) have shown that, while castration has no significant effect on the longevity of male dogs, it tends to increase the life span of bitches from 11 to 11.9 years. It has been suggested (P. Holt, 'Early neutering of dogs', *Vet Rec.*, 2 December 2000) that bitches should not be neutered before their first season if they show signs of juvenile vaginitis, infantile vulva, urinary incontinence or if they are of a breed disposed to urethral sphincter mechanism incontinence. Juvenile vaginitis and infantile vulva usually right themselves at the first season, but are likely to persist if a bitch is neutered before her first season, and, in the case of sphincter mechanism incompetence, a dog may become incontinent if it is neutered before this. Furthermore, neutering before the first season may give rise to urinary incontinence. A study (M.V. Thrusfield, 'Association between urinary incontinence and spaying in bitches', *Vet Rec.*, 29 June 1985) found that of 3,260 bitches, 5.7 per cent of the spayed ones examined had urinary incontinence, whereas only 1.2 per cent of all the bitches examined were incontinent. Spaying appears to increase the likelihood of incontinence almost fivefold. It may also induce a permanent state of pseudopregnancy (M.J.A. Harvey *et al.*, 'A study of the aetiology of pseudopregnancy in the bitch and the effect of cabergoline therapy', *Vet. Rec.*, 17 April 1999).

Salpingectomy

This is a procedure that involves the removal of a small section of the oviduct and the cauterizing of the ends. The uterus and the ovaries are left intact, and so the bitch, though infertile, still comes into season and is not deprived of the effects that the organs produce.

Vasectomy

Veterinary surgeons have been able to perform vasectomy as an alternative to castration for about twenty years, yet few offer this as an alternative or discuss it with their clients, nor do texts that purport to offer advice to owners draw attention to vasectomy as an alternative, possibly a preferable one to castration, and neither do welfare organizations so much as mention vasectomy as a less traumatic procedure than castration but which has similar consequences without the possible side effects sometimes associated with castration.

Contraception

It should surely be unnecessary to insist, given that all other things are equal, that the best form of contraception is to keep fertile dogs well away from bitches when they are in season. Owners, however, should appreciate that both dogs and bitches are incredibly resourceful at this time and may find a way through, over or under obstacles that have previously been regarded as impregnable. Street-wise roaming dogs will locate in-season bitches, particularly when these have been exercised along the public highway, will gather at the opportune time and will each do their utmost to mate the bitch, who will herself do whatever she can to encourage and help. It is not unknown for matings to take place through a chain link fence.

If, for some reason, it may not be possible to avoid conception, contraception that avoids the need for surgery would appear to be the next choice, with surgery that is least invasive the next, and deeply invasive surgery used only when all other options are deemed inappropriate. If fact, both the veterinary profession and welfare agencies strongly prefer the last option almost to the exclusion of all others.

Pharmaceutical Contraception

For some years veterinary pharmaceutical products that suppress or postpone oestrus have been available in Britain. They have been extensively used without untoward effects by owners who want to compete with bitches that might be perform less well or distract others if they were in season. More recently, products have been licensed in both the USA and Australia that have the effect of making dogs temporarily or permanently and irreversibly infertile. Products based on deslorelin acetate produce infertility of about six months' duration. Zinc gluconate-based injections given to dogs at three to ten months of age have the effect of atrophying the testes and so produce permanent, irreversible infertility. Implants that do this are being used to calm sexually-induced aggression. All these avoid the need for any surgery and thus the risks and side effects attendant on surgery. They should also provide a far cheaper alternative to any neutering procedure that involves surgery.

Responsible Breeding

One of the most important ways of protecting dogs from inherited disease, from a lack of resistance to infectious disease and for having their lives shortened by avoidable conditions arises out of the efforts of responsible breeders. The Kennel Club, in association with the British Small Animals Veterinary Association, supports a number of schemes to test the genetic health of all breeds in general and of some breeds in particular. Schemes aimed at specific inherited diseases include von Willebrand's disease (vWD), copper toxicosis, hip dysplasia, elbow dysplasia and several eye diseases. In addition, the Kennel Club Health Foundation Fund, part of the Kennel Club Charitable Trust, assists breed clubs to carry out the research that will help them to exert effective control over inherited diseases.

Choke Chains

Formerly used, often in association with a peremptory shriek of 'Walkies', as an aid to training but now discredited; aggression may even be made worse by their use. Choke chains pulled with sufficient vigour may inflict spinal damage on a dog and even with less vigour may damage a dog's throat.

Confinement

If they have a mind to do so, almost any dog, but especially the terrier breeds that remain close to their working roots, can get over, through or under almost any obstacle they may encounter. Even the most securely fenced garden can be made insecure if thoughtless visitors, of which delivery people and untrained children are the worst culprits, leave gates open.

Fencing

In order to attain a worthwhile level of security, fencing must be sufficiently high to prevent dogs from jumping or climbing over it. It should be buried to prevent dogs that prefer to tunnel to freedom rather than to jump and should be stout enough to deter even a determined chewer and its apertures small enough to prevent a dog from squeezing through.

Electric Fencing

Although electric fencing is considered as a perfectly acceptable way of keeping farm stock within bounds, its use is generally not regarded as appropriate for dogs. Welfare agencies, the Kennel Club and some veterinary surgeons are implacably opposed to its use. It operates through a buried electrified cable that transmits a mild shock through a collar worn by dogs within its perimeter. The dogs quickly learn to avoid the cable and so can be regarded as secure. Animals not wearing a collar can cross the cable with impunity. It thus does not act as a deterrent to wild life nor, unfortunately, to wandering dogs or cats.

Kennels

If dogs are to be housed outside the house, kennels with a covered run will provide good accommodation if they are well lined, warm, dry and sufficiently large to provide a reasonable amount of space. An adjoining run, whether roofed or not, will provide more accommodation and a degree of variety. Kennels need to have sufficient head room to allow the owner to clean them in comfort and have an impervious floor that can be washed easily. They should also be capable of being made secure, and if a garage alarm can be installed then so much the better. Do not site kennels under trees or in places in which they will not get any sunlight; conversely, do not place them where they will receive the full heat of the sun. Our own species is comfortable in a temperature of between 18° and 21°C (64°–70°F), dogs prefer a slightly lower temperature of about 13°C (55°F) and some, particularly breeds of northern origin, are quite content curled up in show and at temperatures at or even below freezing. Ventilation is important in order to keep the environment wholesome; five air changes per hour should be regarded as ideal. Noisy kennels are not only stressful for the dogs but also for those who may have to spend an appreciable length of time in them.

Muzzles

Seldom, if ever, are muzzles needed by companion dogs although they are always required for racing hounds. Aggressive dogs or dogs that are not to be trusted among any other creatures will be prevented from doing damage and will be easier to control and train.

Runs

Runs may do no more than provide a secure place in which a dog can enjoy a period of solitude, or they may be large enough for dogs to exercise themselves. A small run needs to be paved, not just so that it can be cleaned but also so that it will not be permanently muddy during wet weather. One advantage of a small run, suitable for one or two small dogs, is that it can easily be moved and, with a fabric cover to provide both shade and some degree of protection on windy days, is adaptable to changing requirements. Even larger, well-mown grass runs need to be rested from time to time in order to prevent the build up of parasites and infectious organisms.

Restraints

The law requires that all dogs should wear a collar with a tag that identifies both the dog and its owner. The law is of considerable assistance to thieves and would-be thieves and for that reason, as well as because the majority are unaware of the requirement, owners largely ignore it.

Names

Every Kennel Club-registered dog will have a name by which it is registered. Most breeders have an affix, a kennel name, attached to all the puppies they breed; to this will be added one or two others to form a unique label for the dog. Use of the registered name is usually confined to official purposes. Some breeders, especially if the puppy is more than just a few weeks old, may give it a name that it will have learned to recognize. If this name does not appeal it can easily be changed. Giving a dog a name that it will quickly learn to recognize, which is appropriate to the breed and which the owner can call without embarrassment, should be a priority to be considered even before the puppy arrives at its new home. Try to avoid names that are obvious or commemorate some pop star whose fame is likely to be outlived by the dog, and avoid the crass humour that will cease to be amusing after a week or two: a simple one- or two-syllable name will be preferable.

11   Basic Training

Dog training as a livelihood is not, as some might suppose, a recent arrival on the scene. In 1685 John Harris, a yeoman of Willdon, in the parish of Hastlebury, in Worcestershire, entered into an agreement with Henry Herbert of Ribbesford to train a Spaniel bitch for a fee of 30 shillings. The agreement was set with care and in detail:

> I will from the day of the date hereof, untill the first day of March next, well and sufficiently mayntayne and keepe a Spanill bitch named Quaud, this day [7 October 1685] delivered into my custody by the said Henry Herbert, and will before the said first day of March next, well and effectually traine up and teach the said bitch to sitt partridges, pheasants, and other game, as well and exactly as the best sitting dogges usually sett the same. And the said bitch, so trayned and taught, shall and will delivere to the said Henry Herbert, or whom he shall appoint to receive her, att his house in Ribbesford aforesaid, on the first day of March next. And if at any time after the said bitch shall for want of use or practise, or otherwise, forgett to sett game aforesaid I will at my costes and charges mayntayne her a month or longer, as often as need shall require, to trayne up and teach her to sett game aforesaid, and shall and will fully and effectually teach her to sett game as well and exactly as it is above mentyon'd.

Training a dog to compete successfully in any of the competitive activities authorized by the Kennel Club is first a matter of making the right choice of breed and bloodlines. Secondly, it is a matter that is reliant on the skill of the trainer. To train a dog to a high level calls for skill, patience, determination and experience. However, all dogs need to absorb some degree of basic training if they are to grow into good family companions.

The New Puppy

The first lessons a puppy must learn are often those that teach it to lead a happy life independent of other dogs and, for short periods, to accept isolation. It requires no more than a few moments thought to appreciate the adjustment required of a puppy when it is first taken from its litter mates and a familiar home and routine. When a puppy leaves the place of its birth it will be frightened and bewildered for a time. It will probably be taken to its new home in a car and may not previously have travelled in this way. If it is not actually sick it may well dribble, and if it is travelling on its new owner's knee something to provide protection against sickness is essential. If the puppy is very small it might be carried in a cardboard box, or, if the new owner is well prepared, in a suitable travelling cage that will also serve when it is adult.

The transition from its place of birth to a new home will be eased if something that carries the familiar scent and feel makes the move with it. Some breeders will supply a small piece of bedding and most will happily

Ready for a game.

familiarize the puppy with a soft toy, towel or some piece of fabric supplied by the prospective owner that can go with the puppy to its new home. Some breeders will also suggest wrapping an alarm clock in a towel in order that the puppy may be reassured by its ticking; a radio might serve the same purpose. It is to be expected that the puppy will be apprehensive during its first few days in a new home; it may signal its fears by howling or refusing to eat. Opinions vary as to whether a puppy should be left alone to become accustomed to its solitary situation or whether it is better to ease its fears by taking it into the bedroom. A new puppy should be provided with a space in which its bed is situated and in which it is secure and has its privacy respected by all members of the household. Children should

be taught that the puppy is not merely a plaything but, just like them, has needs of its own. These include the need to sleep. It is convenient if there is room in the house for a playpen situated on an impervious floor lined with newspaper and containing the puppy's bed, toys and a drinking bowl.

A few minutes playing with the new owner and being encouraged to come to call will be enjoyed by the puppy and enable another small step to be taken in its training. A puppy may be fearful of approaching a standing person who looms over him but may be less fearful if the person crouches to something closer to its own level.

New Ideas on Training

In recent years the attitudes of many self-proclaimed experts on the training of dogs have undergone considerable change. Those who are able to ignore a new puppy's cries and can leave it to come to terms with its new situation are perhaps harking back to the bad old days when dogs were trained by having their will and resistance 'broken'. The idea that dogs must be 'broken' may now be a thing of the past but the idea has resurfaced in slightly different terms: now the talk is of 'dominance' and the need for owners to assert and maintain their own dominance. This need is even extended so far as to suggest that a dog that sleeps on its owner's bed is doing so in order to exert its own dominance. The same preposterous idea is also applied to the need for owners to insist that they and not their dog pass through doors first.

The avoidance of a dominating dog has given rise to the suggestion that a dog must not be fed before its owner eats. If owner and dog were eating from the same platter the suggestion might have something to commend it, but to allow a dog to remain hungry while the owner tucks into his food seems

Dogs should be introduced to other species as part of their basic education.

almost cruel. Healthy dogs of all ages get excited at the prospect of a meal. Once they have been fed and exercised the need to importune the owner in the hope of relieving their hunger will no longer be a factor in their behaviour. If they are permitted to remain with their owner during his meal is a matter for the owner to decide, but they should only be allowed to do so on the strict condition that they do not beg for food nor importune other family members or guests. Good behaviour might, when the meal has ended, be rewarded with a titbit.

Settling In

The first thing a dog needs to learn is its name, constant repetition of which, accompanied by praise and reward when it responds, will take no more than a day or two if the dog and its owner are moderately intelligent.

The first two stages of training a young puppy are most often house training and preventing it from chewing.

House Training

My wife and I had some high words upon my telling her that I would fling the dog which her brother gave her out of the window if he pissed the house any more.

Samuel Pepys, *Diary*, 12 February 1660

Most breeds respond readily and quickly to their owner's insistence that they must excrete only out of doors. Indeed, such behaviour may become so ingrained that a bout of uncontrollable diarrhoea or incontinence may result in the dog's suffering from what seems remarkably close to guilt.

It is advisable to feed a new puppy in a secure run if the garden is not completely escape-proof, and, in any case, preferably under supervision out of doors. Not only do puppies eat more frequently than an adult, but, like a human baby, also pass excrement more frequently and more urgently. If a puppy is fed out of doors it will, given the opportunity, quickly learn to defecate soon after it has eaten. If the owner watches for the signs that usually precede this, hyperactive sniffing at various suitable places, turning in circles, arching the back and straining, the behaviour can be verbally encouraged so that the dog will learn to defecate almost on command.

Whenever a dog is exercised in a public place such as on a grass verge or in a public park the owner should be equipped to remove any excrement that may be deposited by his dog. A plastic bag pulled over the hand can be used to pick up the offending material that can then be deposited in a suitable place. Some local authorities provide special bins for this purpose and even those who do not do so have the right, increasingly often used, to fine an offending owner.

Chewing

Puppies begin to discard milk teeth at about sixteen weeks of age. In order to speed the process, as well as to seek to relieve some of the discomfort, they will often seek out objects that they can chew. They may also do it as a means to explore the taste and texture of unfamiliar objects and to relieve boredom; in this respect they behave very like human babies and the solution to the problem is much the same: give the puppy something it will enjoy chewing but which will not harm it nor give rise to any consternation in the household.

Grooming

Although the puppy may have no need of being groomed, a few minutes spent combing or brushing it will begin to accustom it to a routine that should be performed regularly and thoroughly throughout its life. The exercise helps to establish a bond between puppy and owner, much as would a wild, female canine establish a bond with her offspring by licking and cleaning them. It also provides an opportunity to check for signs of ill health, on the eruption of teeth and, especially if the puppy is destined for a

Confidence without aggression is essential to success in the show ring.

126

career in the show ring, to begin the training that will accustom it to being thoroughly examined.

Collars

Once the puppy has settled into its new home it should be equipped with a soft, lightweight collar. Some will take no notice of the new experience, others will make efforts to rid themselves of the encumbrance and yet others will initially display a reluctance to move as though the collar somehow prevented them from doing so. Once the puppy has become accustomed to the collar a light lead may be attached and the puppy gently encouraged to take a walk round the garden. It is unlikely to understand what is expected of it immediately but will soon realize what it is. Some years ago, the idea was popularized by a television performer that a dog equipped with a choke chain to which was attached a stout lead by which the handler could direct sharp, constricting jerks at the dog's throat could, with the accompaniment of shrill cries of 'Walkies', be trained to the lead in a matter of minutes. Happily a more enlightened attitude now prevails. Choke chains, harsh treatment and shrieks have no place in the training of any dog (*see* below).

Retrieving

One accomplishment that all owners should teach their dog is to retrieve. Chasing a thrown object and bringing it back to its owner is an excellent form of exercise and a considerable source of fun. Some dogs, especially of breeds bred to retrieve game, are naturals and never happier than when carrying some thing they have picked up while at exercise. Other breeds may take a while before they begin to appreciate that a toy thrown by their owner can be chased and picked up, and that if it is then returned to its owner the game can continue. A well behaved dog is not only more enjoyable to own than an unruly beast whose every desire is pandered to by an indulgent owner, but is also a source of pride that demonstrates that the owner is patient, knowledgeable and responsible.

Ranking

A well-reared and well-socialized puppy will be inquisitive and manipulative. Training a puppy involves a degree of negotiation between puppy and owner with each attempting to find ways of bending the other to its will. If a fair balance is not achieved and the puppy becomes dominant over the owner it will be far less pleasure and trouble to own. A confident puppy will continually test and seek to extend the limits of what is allowable. It in some respects the puppy will be attempting to train its owner, just as its owner will be trying to train it. Training is a matter first of selecting a dog that is likely to be susceptible to the process and then diverting its inbred inclinations to the owner's will. Given only the slightest degree of encouragement an intelligent dog will quickly train its owners in how best to satisfy its wishes.

If the now popular view that dogs regard themselves and their owner's family as part of the same pack is not seriously flawed, the dog will tend to become the omega, the lowest ranking member of that pack and will regard the dominant person in the household as the alpha-ranking individual. It may well be that dogs decide for themselves whether the dominant person is male or female, and this may explain why some dogs prefer men to women or, more likely, the other way round. Children in the household may be seen as of low rank and, when that rank is seen by the dog as lower than its own, the dog may seek to exert its dominance over them. It may be disobedient and

Even with a small boy to play with, overfeeding can lead to obesity and ill-health in a sedentary dog.

even aggressive towards them in order to establish its own higher rank. This situation is best avoided by training children to respect the dog and to use their authority fairly and wisely.

Punishment

let me ... impress upon those who break or train the dog, that they are never so likely to bring out his good qualities as when they are gaining his confidence by kindness, and stimulating him to fresh exertions of his wonderful brain by encouragement and rewards. Punishment is always perilous.

The Dog: with Simple Directions for His Treatment, Thomas Pearce, Idstone, 1872

The days when training was, quite literally, a matter of breaking a dog's will by beating it into submission and of making it servile to its owner's will are now consigned to the past. The process too often destroyed the dog's individuality, eroded its initiative and turned it into something almost akin to a robot. Current training regimes utilize a dog's inherent abilities and curiosity and reward desirable behaviour. (But if a dog finds that it can get its own way by barking, soiling it bed or in the house or by some other inappropriate behaviour it will quickly learn to exploit the situation.)

Although physical punishment is now largely a practice of the past, lessons are to be learned by considering its effect. The use of a whip, stick or, in some ways the worst option, a rolled-up newspaper, is seldom, if ever, justified. The excuse put forward for the last is that it does not inflict pain but that the dog quickly associates the loud noise it makes with punishment. Whether or not pain is inflicted is surely open to doubt, but to teach a dog to associate punishment with a loud noise is both cruel and asinine. Huntsmen may occasionally use a whip, not so much to inflict a thrashing, but to control a recalcitrant individual hound that is otherwise beyond reach and to give it a sharp reminder that its behaviour is undesirable. Knowing hounds quickly learn to modify their behaviour whenever the butt of the whip is pointed at them. The use of a stick is beyond the pale because far more humane alternatives are available.

Nowadays, with a better understanding of canine behaviour and a more humane attitude towards dogs, punishment of unacceptable behaviour has been largely replaced by reward for and encouragement of good behaviour. The process is based on a dog's confidence in and trust of its owner, in the reliance it has on its owner's ability to make consistent and fair demands that it can understand. The dog must be able to associate rewards with desirable behaviour and their withholding with undesirable behaviour. A dog must be able to recognize why it is being rewarded or rewards are being withheld. If it is unable to do so, the wrong sort of behaviour could be reinforced and the attempt to train it become counterproductive. Rewarding desirable behaviour may take the form of a physical reward or of praise. If rewards are withheld, the dog should be praised as soon as its behaviour conforms to its owner's wishes. An admonitory finger accompanied by verbal recrimination uttered in a threatening but not loud tone is as far as punishment need go other than in the most exceptional circumstances. In most circumstances punishment is not necessary; it suffices if undesirable behaviour is frustrated or better still diverted (for example, if a dog tries to jump up at its owner this can be frustrated simply by putting a knee in its way). But reward and correction must be immediate and not delayed until the dog is unable to associate its own behaviour with the consequences of it. The basic flaw is that the means of punishment may not always be to hand.

Fights

From time to time a dog may take exception to another, much as we might with people who we dislike. Once the problem is recognized the sensible course is to ensure that the two dogs are never able to express their hostility. Some gladiatorial breeds are ruthless fighters, partly because of their impressive strength and partly because they appear to have lost the ability to submit to an aggressor or to recognize submission in another dog. Such dogs should be kept under close control when in the company of dogs they do not know.

If dogs do become involved in a fight, or seem to be about to do so, difficult though it may be, the handler should remain calm and quiet, nothing is better calculated to start a fight than a handler who is shouting and screaming but doing nothing effective to keep the potential combatants apart. Being given a peremptory order by its owner or by the owner's seeming to leave the scene might divert a dog. If a fight begins, hitting the dogs will encourage aggression; they might be separated by using a yard brush or, if they are quite small, by lifting them from the ground and hanging them over a fence or gate so that, when they relax their grip, they will fall on different sides of the obstacle. Choking them by using the lead as a ligature will restrict breathing and may cause them to release their grip. Pulling at the leads will achieve nothing other than make any injuries far worse than they might have been, while kicking or hitting the dogs will simply excite them still more and may also cause injury. The use of buckets of water or a hosepipe may also deter them from further aggression, but once the 'red mist' has descended the dogs should be kept well apart as soon as they are released.

Even in the best-regulated families squabbles may occur. Hormonal imbalance, seeking a higher status within the pack hierarchy and jealousy are only some of the reasons why two dogs in the same household may fight. Such dogs may be controlled but should not be trusted together without supervision.

Commands

Heeling
Training a dog to walk at heel cannot begin until the dog has been taught to walk on a lead. Puppies often resent the restriction and will do their utmost to escape. They should be accustomed to wearing a collar and only

Walking at heel.

Teaching to stay.

Teaching to sit.

when they have accepted this should they have a light lead attached to it. The dog should be encouraged to follow by using rewards and praise and, when it has learned to accept and respect the control imposed on it by the lead, it can begin to walk at heel. The lead should be shortened and the dog prevented from running ahead.

Sit

By using the lead to raise a dog's head and the other hand to manoeuvre it gently into a sitting position, the dog may be made to sit. The exercise should be accompanied by repetition of the order to sit and by a hand signal – an open palm is convenient, and followed by reward and praise. Frequent repletion but never so prolonged that the dog becomes bored will soon teach the lesson.

Stay

Once a dog has been taught to sit on command it should be told to stay, the owner retreating to the full extent of a fairly long lead, repeating the order and reinforcing it with the open palm hand signal. By slowly increasing the length of time the dog is required to remain unmoved and by increasing the distance between owner and dog, the stage will be reached when the owner may briefly move out of sight. Success calls for praise and reward.

The down position.

The sit at heel.

Down

Once a dog has been taught to sit, the lead may be used to lower its forequarters so that it is lying down, the exercise being accompanied by the appropriate order and signal, and success being rewarded and praised.

Come

It is important that the dog should return to its owner on command and teaching it to do so. should form part of its early education. By moving slightly away from the dog or attracting its attention when it is at a distance, the dog will soon learn to associate the command with the prospect of reward and praise and will return to the owner to collect its dues. The appropriate order and hand signal given by the owner, especially from a squatting and less dominant position, will quickly become associated with its purpose. Never ask a dog to 'Come' and, when it does so, punish or subject it to something it may find unpleasant. Praise and reward are important.

12   Travel

International Travel

A few breeds seem disposed to show signs of physical and mental distress when travelling, but the vast majority of dogs accept journeys without any signs of being distressed; indeed, some seem almost to be disappointed if they are not allowed to accompany their owner on each and every journey. The situation is no different than that which pertains in our own species.

The government's plan for implementing its animal health and welfare strategy was published by DEFRA at the end of 2003. It discussed plans to implement the EC regulations on pet travel and noted that the United Kingdom's defences against rabies need to be maintained, but made no mention of any other diseases that might enter the country as a consequence of the inadequate surveillance of animals entering or returning to Britain from countries in which exotic diseases may be endemic.

These currently include bartonellosis, borreliosis, canine subcutaneous dirofilariosis, canine ehrlichiosis (canine rickettsiosis), Echinococcus multilocularis, hepatozoonosis, visceral leishmaniasis, *Babesia canis* and *Brucella canis*; it is likely that the passage of time will extend the list. These are not minor illnesses, but some that are dangerous to dogs and cats as well as to people and which may even be life-threatening. We are talking about diseases that are not easy to treat and will, if they become established in Britain, place an additional load on NHS resources. The diseases mentioned by the Department of Environment, Food and Rural Affairs (DEFRA) are leishmaniosis, ehrlichiosis, babesiosis and dirofilariosis. They could also have added hepatoozoonosis, borreliosis and tickborne encephalitis to the list.

In a discussion staged at the Edinburgh BVA Congress, Chris Laurence, veterinary director of the Dogs' Trust (formerly and more familiarly known as the NCDL), expressed the view that PETS had originally been introduced to aid people who worked overseas to take their animals with them. It was not, he said, designed for the leisure industry, allowing people to take their pet for a two-week holiday. He did not mention the use of PETS to enable show competitors to take dogs overseas for period appreciably less than two weeks; but did, however, express the view that the welfare of some animals, taken from Britain to a climate, which was 15 or 20° warmer, into unfamiliar surroundings and by an owner who might not be aware of the restrictions imposed on dogs in that country, could thereby be compromised. He criticized that lack of a mandatory surveillance scheme that meant that, while large numbers of dog had entered this country as a result of PETS, there was no means of monitoring what happened to them subsequently. 'The greatest risk from PETS', he said, 'comes from the ignorance of the average owner taking their dog overseas.' PETS provided an example of legislation that might compromise welfare for political ends.

As a result of this and other reservations, DEFRA set up a surveillance scheme intended to discover what exotic diseases were being treated in veterinary surgeries up and down the country. That the scheme relies on the voluntary input by veterinary surgeons and is financially supported entirely by them and at a difficult time for them, it may produce some worthwhile information ... An announcement was made in February 2003 that a scheme known as DACTARI (Dog and Cat Travel and Risk Information) was to be set up and that it would be reviewed in six months' time to see whether it should continue; over a year later no further mention on DEFRA's websites was to be found.

Imported Diseases

I hesitate to give the benefit of the doubt to the new systems intended to keep rabies out of Britain, the best I can do is to hope that they achieve their intended purpose. What I cannot do is feel confident that the new systems will not open the doors to a number of diseases, including potentially fatal zoonoses, not now present in this country.

Pet owners would be right to be concerned about the future health of their animals, whether or not they have journeyed overseas, and should also be concerned about their own health. In the past, quarantine played its part, largely unrecognized, in keeping these diseases out of Britain. They were assisted by a climate that was inhospitable to many of the diseases, at least some of which require a Mediterranean climate in which to thrive. Nowadays global warming may create more suitable conditions.

To further complicate the matter, the possibility that hunting may be banned will get rid of a method of controlling foxes, which now exists at no cost to the country at large. It is fair to say that it even contrives, directly and indirectly, to produce income for the government. All other methods of control, no matter how desirable they may

be in other respects, can be carried out only at a cost to government. In continental Europe the control of foxes by means of the aerial distribution of vaccine capsules has, at considerable and on-going cost, achieved appreciable success. That success, however, has been at the expense of an increase in fox tapeworm, echinococcus multilocularis, which is not found in Britain but is now prevalent in continental urban fox populations, which in humans gives rise to helminth infection with a 95 per cent mortality rate within 10 to 15 years. No effective vaccine is yet available.

A number of vector-borne infections are prevalent in Europe, especially round the Mediterranean. They include tick-borne babesiosis and ehrlichiosis, mosquito-borne heartworm and leishmaniasis, transmitted by phlebotomine sand flies. Surveys have demonstrated that some of these infections are carried by almost half the dogs in certain areas of continental Europe. It may already be too late to prevent these infections from becoming established in Britain; to prevent them from doing so will require constant and informed scrutiny at ports of entry as well as by the veterinary profession. Such measures cannot be carried out other than at appreciable cost to the public at large and to pet owners in particular.

National Travel

Whenever we sell a puppy we make an effort to try to persuade the new owner to buy a cage so that the dog can travel by car in greater safety and has a place to sleep in with which it is familiar when it is away from home. I do not think that our efforts are wholly successful; indeed, some new owners react quite strongly against the idea of caging their dog. They regard such a practice as cruel. Of course, a cage is not appropriate to every breed, sometimes a well-secured dog guard might be better and some people (I am not one of them) regard a harness as adequate.

The purpose of all these devices is to protect the dog from injury or from injuring other occupants, should the car be involved in an accident. They also prevent dogs from escaping from a damaged car and becoming a source of danger to other road users. A cage also prevents dogs from chewing the upholstery or Aunt Edith's hat. Muddy paws do not leave their imprint all over the car. (I had not myself realized that the Highway Code insists that all animals in vehicles should be restrained in some appropriate way. Their recommendations are more often ignored than not.)

Kennels and Other Forms of Accommodation

Many dog owners choose not to take their dogs with them when they go on holiday or are away from home for a few days. There are a number of ways of accommodating dogs in these circumstances. Owners may invite a friend or professional 'dog sitter' to stay in their home in order to provide care for the dogs; such arrangements are often highly satisfactory, provided that the person in charge is trustworthy, knowledgeable and acceptable to the dogs. It is essential that the situation be fully covered by appropriate insurance.

The most common method of providing dogs with care and accommodation is in boarding kennels. These vary between the very good and the truly awful, yet many owners take their quality on trust and consign their dogs to their mercies without a moments thought. About 16 per cent of those who use boarding kennels visit them before to placing their pet there. Of these, only about 28 per cent bothered to check that the kennels were properly licensed and

only 16 per cent checked that the kennels were properly insured. Potential customers should ensure that their dog will be provided with adequate and appropriate exercise during its stay and not be left confined in a small cell. They should also seek assurance about whether or not it will share its accommodation with another dog. It is not unknown for unscrupulous kennel owners to show good accommodation and, as soon as the owners have departed, to move the dog into less salubrious accommodation.

These facilities are all supposed to be subject to regular inspection by local authority officials, but the quality of inspection is highly variable. It is far better to rely on the recommendation of satisfied customers and personal inspection.

Some local authorities publish standards, often based on WHO recommendations, which licensed boarding kennels are expected to maintain. These may differ slightly, but the basic requirements tend to be much the same: all kennels must have heating capable of providing a temperature suitable for the requirements of each dog and to maintain sleeping areas at a minimum of 10°C (50°F). There must be heated isolation facilities appropriate to the needs of sick dogs.

All kennels, corridors and exercise areas must be clean, free from accumulations of dust or dirt and kept in a manner that will reduce the risk of disease and provide for the comfort of animals. Each occupied kennel must be thoroughly cleaned at least once daily, and all excreta and soiled material removed from areas to which dogs might have access. Facilities must be available for the proper reception, storage and disposal of waste matter. Clinical waste arising out of the treatment of sick animals must be stored and disposed of in accordance with the appropriate legislation. All bedding areas must be kept clean and dry. When kennels are vacated, they and all bedding must be thoroughly cleaned, disinfected and dried before being occupied by another dog. Measures must be taken to prevent the ingress of rodents, insects and other pests to all areas within the establishment.

The WHO recommendations were intended to reduce human health risks associated with animals in urban areas and so do not fully address the needs of the animals themselves, especially in terms of the size of enclosures and exercise paddocks and how much exercise should be given. Obviously, dogs need an enclosure of adequate size in which to spend the time when they are not at exercise. Both pens and exercise paddocks must be within secure enclosures. All dogs must be supplied with adequate and suitable food, fresh, wholesome drinking water must be available at all times and all utensils maintained in a thoroughly clean and disinfected condition to prevent cross-contamination. Kitchen, food preparation and food-storage facilities must be maintained in a clean condition, and food storage must be proof against insects and other pests. Hot and cold water must be provided for washing food equipment, eating and drinking vessels, and a separate hand basin with hot and cold water be available for the use of staff.

Precautions must be taken to prevent infection or contagious disease and eliminate parasites. Many licensing authorities insist that all dogs should have been vaccinated against canine distemper, infectious canine hepatitis, leptospirosis, parvovirus and other diseases. Evidence that might be provided by blood tests that immunity levels are adequate and in accordance with a routine that is in some cases contrary to manufacturers' recommendations must be provided, although there is seldom a requirement that ensures that the evidence provided is for the dogs in question.

13 Activities

In shapes and forms of dogges; of which there are but two sorts that are usefull for man's profit, which are the mastiffe and the little whippet, or house dogge; all the rest are for pleasure and recreations.

John Taylor, *All the Workes of John Taylor, the Water Poet* (1603)

Introduction

It is difficult to think of any range of activities competitive, educational and social that cater for both young and old that were not made available as a result of an interest in dogs. For thousands of years, dogs have been hunting companions, guards and social companions, whose beauty, intelligence, obedience and speed have been a source of pride for their owners. In recent years what might be seen as traditional roles have been extended in ways that are both surprising and beneficial to man.

In Britain, the Kennel Club, a private club with a limit of 1,500 elected members, regulates the majority of canine activities. It was founded in 1873 in order to regularize the increasing number of competitions involving dogs, as well as the growing interest in breeding them. Then and now its authority stems entirely from the willing acceptance of the majority of people who are interested in dogs. As a consequence, it is regarded as the primary source of information and influence on matters related to them – by government, by welfare organizations and by the veterinary profession. In 2002 the Club registered 226,318 dogs and licensed 3,252 events. From time to time attempts are made to create rival organizations, some are intent on personal gain and others on a desire to avoid Kennel Club authority. All rely heavily on the Club for credible breed standards, rules that govern competitions and the authenticity of information on which competitions are based. These other organizations have nothing of value to contribute to dog owners, are ignored by legitimate breeders and should be avoided by potential dog owners.

The activities in which owners and their dogs may take part include many of a competitive nature as well as those that have social value. Interest in dogs may generate intellectual curiosity that throws light on the attitudes of our predecessors as well as help to inform our own. Nor should sporting activities be ignored: they too have social value in binding rural communities and bringing urban dwellers in touch with country pursuits. Some of these activities are now under threat from those who believe that they have no place in a modern society. Not all these people understand or are knowledgeable about what they oppose or of the effect of that opposition. Nevertheless, their opposition is genuine and must be heeded. From a historical viewpoint, it would be regrettable if some long-established activities

Success at a show should be enjoyable.

were to be outlawed; the welfare, social or economic aspects of them should be acknowledged.

Some activities require considerable levels of skill, physical prowess and dedication, while others rely on a social conscience and a desire to help others. They provide interest for all members of society, rich and poor, young and old, male and female and an opportunity for social contact between people of all ages and from every stratum of society to indulge their particular interest, for teams as well as for individuals. The richness of the social mix is perhaps one reason for its extraordinary diversity. Some take place close to home while others may call for trips overseas. It would be difficult to find any other range of interests that is quite so inclusive as those that derive from an interest in dogs. Virtually all dog-related competitive activities exist at different levels that reflect the skill and aspiration of the competitors, in spite of the general lack of interest by the media in them.

Agility

Agility competitions include matches in which entry is confined to members of a society, limited events for members of a show society or who are resident within a particular area, open events available to all competitors, and championship show events at which agility certificates may be won. Classes are available for standard dogs over 432mm (18in) at the withers, midi-dogs between 432 and 381mm (18–15in) at the withers and mini-dogs, under 381mm (15in) at the withers. Classes are arranged in a rising standard of difficulty, from elementary, starters, novice, intermediate, seniors, advanced, open and championship. Competitions take place within a test area 32m (105ft) square, which may contain a variety of obstacles, including hurdle, rising spread jump, brush fence, hoop, table, long jump, water jump, wishing well or lych gate, collapsible tunnel, pipe tunnel, weaving poles, pause box, 'A' ramp, see-saw, dog walk and cross over.

Bloodhound Trials

It goes without saying that the basic requirement of this activity is to own or at least have access to a Bloodhound. Hounds are leashed and only those hunted free that hold a working permit and are certified steady with farm stock. They are set to follow a line, an artificial scent trail; novice stakes involve a 1.6km-long trail (1 mile), not less than half an hour cold, that is to say, laid not less than half an hour before to the start of the competition. Junior stakes involve a trail 3.2km (2 miles) long and not less than half an hour cold; and intermediate stakes are run over 4.0km (2.5 miles), with a trail not less than one and a half hours cold; and senior stakes over a 4.8km (3 miles) trail (not less than two hours cold).

Breeding

It is not within the scope of this book to discuss the complexities of breeding. Nevertheless, for great many owners breeding dogs is a fascinating hobby that calls for extensive knowledge and skills. It is physically and emotionally demanding but immensely rewarding. People, who have never previously owned a dog, may decide that they would like to breed a litter of puppies. The reasons for doing so vary. Some want to perpetuate the qualities of a much-loved pet, others may want to try to recoup some of the cost of buying their dog or even to make a profit and yet others may regard the process as a good way of educating children about the reproductive process. A few will have

decided that they want to breed dogs as a hobby. Whatever the motives, the process is the same and should never be embarked upon unless the bitch is a top-quality representative of her breed, in the prime of life, fit and healthy.

Not everyone is familiar with what is involved. One prospective breeder who wanted a litter of three puppies asked the stud dog's owner whether this meant it was necessary to mate the bitch three times. Another sought to postpone a mating from one weekend to the next that would be more convenient. The breeder accepted the new arrangement only after asking whether it was intended that the bitch should have puppies or simply have sex. Yet another insisted that the bitch should be mated at her own fireside; when the owner of the stud dog arrived to fulfil the tryst, the owner of the bitch had spread a duvet on the hearth and insisted on trying to persuade the bitch to lay on her back. The alarming part of the incident was that the bitch's owner was a doctor. Perhaps breeding a litter of puppies is as useful to adults as it is to children as a means to learn about the reproductive process. Owner's who are thinking of breeding a litter could do worse than consult the author's *Dog Breeding, the Theory and Practice* (The Crowood Press).

Coursing

This is probably the oldest organized competition involving dogs. Lord Orford founded the Swaffham Coursing Society in 1776, although rules had been drawn up by the Duke of Norfolk for King James I of England almost 200 years previously. The rules still follow the pattern established by the Duke. The National Coursing Club now administers the sport. Ground to which hares have been moved, on which they have not been at liberty or which is designed to

A keenly contested class at Crufts.

restrict their complete freedom and liberty during the previous six months is not used. Dogs are released, slipped, in pairs and their performance is judged against their speed: 'Go-bye' in which one dog passes the other, 'Turn' in which the hare's course is changed by at least a right angle, and 'Kill and trip'. Organized coursing is a sport and cannot be justified on utilitarian grounds. Training a hound to the necessary peak of fitness and ability requires a great deal of skill, knowledge and dedication.

Field Trials

Field trials are a competitive exercise intended to assess the working ability of gun dogs in the field working on live, unhandled game and where the game may be shot. Stakes may be run for Retrievers and Irish Water Spaniels, Sporting Spaniels other than Irish Water Spaniels, Pointers and Setters, and other breeds bred to hunt, point and retrieve. Stakes may be open events in which

dogs have the opportunity to qualify as field trial champions, all-aged stakes or novice stakes confined to dogs that have not won at certain levels, and puppy stakes confined to dogs whelped not earlier than 1 January of the previous year.

Flyball

Flyball is the canine competition that allows spectator involvement without demanding any knowledge of dogs or more than a basic understanding of the elementary rules that govern competitions. These take place within an area of not less than 21.34m × 9.14m (70ft × 30ft). Dogs are expected to jump four 30.9cm-high (12in) hurdles in pursuit of tennis balls projected from a box placed at one end of the course.

Heelwork to Music

Exercises set to music are a recent extension of obedience that involve a degree of imagination coupled with choreographical skills and an highly developed ability to train a dog to react to subtle, barely discernible hand signals. Any dog can be trained for the purpose, but competitors who intend to progress to advanced competition should select a breed that has already demonstrated an aptitude. Competitions may involve two categories: heelwork to music in which the dog works off the lead but at the heel of its handler, and freestyle, again based on heelwork off the lead but incorporating movements in any position. Classes may provide for starters, novices, intermediate and advanced depending on the dog's achievements in previous competitions.

Junior Handling

To what extent junior handling enables parents to use their children in order to become involved in a dog-related activity and to what extent it is driven by the enthusiasm of youngsters with an interest in dogs need not be debated here. The best junior handlers attain a high degree of proficiency, in some cases far higher than that by some experienced and successful adult exhibitors. But it must never be forgotten that the purpose of dog shows is not to reward handling ability but to find and reward dogs of outstanding merit.

Racing

Racing may provide enjoyment and exercise for virtually any breed and their owners. It is a frequent ingredient of hunt and working terrier shows, where the competition may be taken very seriously, but where it may also be nothing more than a hilarious way of ending an enjoyable afternoon. Dogs emerge from traps at the start to chase a lure pulled along on a cord attached to a pulley on a static cycle, which an energetic volunteer pedals as

fast as they are able. The lure eventually disappears into a gap between straw bales and the winner is the dog that is first to follow it. The course is usually short and straight but may be made more challenging by the introduction of miniature hurdles. The game is not for the faint-hearted dog or owner and may involve mayhem as dogs vie with one another to catch the lure or to be first to enter the tunnel between the bales.

Much the same system is used for Lurcher racing, although the course is seldom straight and a more sophisticated and far faster lure is employed. Races are split between the several sizes of Lurcher.

Afghan Hounds are trained and sometimes raced on privately owned tracks and very occasionally are raced on public Greyhound tracks. A full-coated Afghan in full flight is an impressive sight, and while it may be slower than a top-class racing Greyhound, the lack of speed is replaced by stamina and enthusiasm.

(The first Greyhound race using an artificial lure was run at the Welsh Harp in 1876; the winner was 'Charming Nell', owned by Edward Dent who bred 'Fullerton', the winner of three Waterloo Cups and who divided another to establish himself as one of the greatest coursing Greyhounds of all time. The event was reported in *The Times*, 11 September 1876, under the heading 'Coursing by Proxy':

> In a field near the Welsh Harp, at Hendon, a course has, in fact, already been laid off for hunting an 'artificial hare'. For distance of 400 yards in a straight line a rail has been laid down in the grass. It is traversed through its whole length by a groove, in which runs an apparatus like a skate on wheels. On this sort of shuttle is mounted the 'artificial hare'. It is made to travel along the ground at any required pace, and so naturally to resemble the living animal that

it is eagerly pursued by Greyhounds. On Saturday afternoon, at half past three o'clock, a trial was made of the new mechanical arrangement. A considerable number of persons were present.

The whole scene was that presented by a racecourse. The rail, over which the sham hare runs, is hid in the grass, and the windlass by which the apparatus is moved does not catch the eye of the spectator. When the hour came all that was seen was the 'artificial hare' bounding out, quite naturally, like the real animal from its bag, followed at once by the hounds like so many kittens after a cork. It was amusing to watch the eager Greyhounds in their headlong race, striving in vain with all their might to overtake the phantom hare, which a touch of the windlass could send spinning like a shadow out of their reach. This new sport is undoubtedly an exciting and interesting one.

But not so exciting and interesting that it would immediately catch public imagination. The track was short and straight and the races over before interest in them could be generated.)

Showing

It is impossible to say when or where the first organized dog show took place. Certainly John Warde, one of the seventeenth century's peripatetic British huntsmen and often described as the 'father' of British foxhunting, was holding organized hound shows on his estate at Squerries, near Westerham in

The spoils of competition can be very impressive.

Kent, at least from 1776. These eventually gave rise to other hound shows in other parts of England, and so, eventually, to the famous Royal Peterborough Hound Show, which not only exists to this day but has become a Mecca for anyone who appreciates working hounds.

Thomas Coke, then aged twenty-two, who had just inherited his father's farms at Holkham in Norfolk, visited Warde's shows. He began to encourage his tenants to adopt the new methods being pioneered by Bakewell, Ellman and others, and to do this ran what would eventually grow into the internationally famous annual Holkham sheep-shearings. Hounds, other sporting dogs and, with Coke's emphasis on sheep farming, some sheep dogs would also be on display, just as they are at many of today's agricultural shows which, in turn, grew out of the Holkham sheep shearings. Who is to say that the idea for these sheep shearings did not spring from Coke's annual visits to Warde's hound shows?

At the same time, a growing concern for the welfare of animals was bringing about opposition to the brutal old baiting sports in which dogs were involved. This coincided with a period of increased industrialization that resulted in a great many people leaving agricultural employment to live in the rapidly growing towns. There they were cut off from all contact with animals and so made good their loss by keeping dogs, not as servants or sporting companions, but as pets. Breeds of dog which had no other purpose but to act as companions became popular and their admirers formed clubs to further and enjoy their mutual interest. These clubs ran small dog shows; one such, almost certainly not the first, was advertised in 1834 and offered a silver cream jug as a prize.

Long before the first dog show took place in Newcastle upon Tyne, rural and urban dog shows were already well established in Britain. However, they were, because of the difficulty of travelling any great distance, of necessity largely local affairs. The Newcastle show was the first to exploit the newly built railways in order to attract exhibitors from further afield, and so could be said to have paved the way for the 7,000 or so events which the Kennel Club now licenses each year, and, less directly, for all the other events which take place in almost every part of the world. Dog shows are not only the most popular competitive activity in which dogs are involved but are also of the greatest interest to the public, with Cruft's the name that everyone if familiar with. In 2003 the hundredth Cruft's Show attracted 20,904 dogs, anything up to 50,000 owners and supporters, 128,998 spectators and well over 200 trade stands over the four days in March when it took place. What a comment on the quality of national newspapers that, even when they deign to notice the event, they seldom get their facts right or reflect the enthusiasm of so many people.

Dogsledding

What has a strong claim to being the greatest test of human and canine endurance takes place in Arctic conditions over the 1,151-mile (1,853km) long Iditarod course from Anchorage to Nome, in Alaska. It was first won in 1973 by Dick Wilmarth's team in 20 days and in 1990, for the fourth time, by Susan Butcher's team in 11 days 1hr 53min, and in 1995 in just 9 days 2hr 42 min 19sec by Doug Swingley's team.

Nothing like it does, or can, take place in Britain, although some British 'mushers' have competed in the Iditarod itself. The nearest things are sledge races in the Highlands. It is, however, illegal to use a dog to draw or help to draw a cart, carriage, truck or barrow on any public highway or other roads over which there is a public right of way. The law is seldom invoked, especially for sled dogs not on the public highway. If it were to be invoked to the letter, it might put doubt on the use of wheels to enable dogs with paralysed rear limbs to be exercised on the public highway.

Terrier Tests

Tests that are intended to discover whether a terrier has retained the ability and desire to work below ground have not yet appeared in Britain. They are, however, popular in other parts of the world, including the United States. It seems likely that they will make their appearance in Britain if hunting is curtailed and the opportunity, already limited, to involve terriers in genuine work is further curtailed.

If artificial terrier tests are ever introduced into Britain, it is to be hoped that they will be based on a more accurate reflection of what terrier work involves than do the American tests. These involve following a trail, something that is not part of terrier work, of entering an artificial earth without hesitation, something that only the most headstrong terrier would do, and of negotiating a tunnel whose internal dimensions are 18in (46cm) square, large enough to accommodate a small terrier man let alone a terrier. Artificial tests require a terrier to face a caged rat, something that would be illegal in Britain, as well as ignoring the fact that working terriers are called upon to face a fox and would be expected when so employed to ignore any other creature.

Obedience

Basic standards of obedience should be taught to every dog, not merely as a matter of discipline and of instilling the owner's dominance, but as a precaution against ill-behaviour and accidents. All dogs are capable of learning the meaning of a few simple commands, although not all owners seem capable of teaching them. Some dogs seem to take a delight in instant obedience and these are the ones that will excel in obedience competitions. Others will obey when only they have nothing more interesting or pressing on their agenda.

As with other competitions, obedience competitions accommodate dogs of different levels of ability, ranging from limited shows at which entry is limited to members of a society, living within a particular locality or to specific breeds, to championship events that are open to all competitors and at which certificates counting towards the title of obedience champion are on offer. Pre-beginners competitions require a dog to walk at heel on a lead, to heel free, to recall from a sitting or down position, to sit for 1min with the handler in sight and to sit for 2min with the handler out of sight. Beginners competitions involve heeling on the lead and free, a recall from the sit or down position, retrieving an article provided by the handler, sitting for 1min with the handler in sight and down for 2min with him out of sight. Novice competitions involve a temperament test in which the dog stands beside the handler and is approached from the front by the judge who runs his hand down the dog's back; any sign of resentment, cringing, growling or snapping is penalized. The dog is then required to heel on a lead and free, to recall from a sit or down position, to retrieve a dumb-bell and to sit for 1min and down for 2min with the handler in sight. Classes become progressively more demanding as the dog progresses through levels A, B and C.

Ringcraft

A number of general canine societies as well as specialized clubs run weekly ringcraft classes. These are intended to accustom show dogs to the atmosphere they will encounter at shows, to mix amicably with other dogs and to become accustomed to the routine of being assessed by the judge. Dogs become accustomed to mixing with others both larger and smaller than themselves, to being examined either on a table or on the floor, to walking smartly around the ring, both alone and with other dogs, and to standing smartly while a final assessment is made by a judge. Some of these classes run a monthly competition in order to test the progress of owners and their dogs, but most place a greater emphasis on education and a strong social element for both owners and dogs. Many will accommodate dogs that are not show prospects, and their owners will derive enjoyment from an evening spent with fellow enthusiasts.

Working Trials

The term is something of a misnomer, in that the ability of dogs to perform the task that the breed came into being to perform is not subject to testing. The tests are the same, with due allowances being made, for all breeds. They involve heel work, sitting, down, recall, retrieving a dumb-bell, sending away and directional control, steadiness to gunshot, speaking on command, agility over clear and long jumps, scaling an obstacle, searching, tracking, quartering the ground, a test of courage, a search for and escorting a 'criminal', recall from 'criminals' and the pursuit and detention of 'criminals.'

Patdogs

A system whereby dogs with reliably friendly temperaments visit people in care homes, long-stay hospitals, secure institutions and the like has existed for a number of years and has given patients comfort and companionship.

Young Kennel Club

The Kennel Club's junior branch provides a range of activities intended to encourage the younger generation to take a responsible interest in dogs. These activities include, for instance, project work, handling competitions and summer camps. During the organization's early days, a nationwide survey was carried out, the first ever, to gather information that would contribute to the limited amount of knowledge then available about latchkey dogs found wandering the streets.

Historical

In recent years the Kennel Club has created the largest European collection of books and sources about dogs. More recently this has been extended to include an art gallery. It is inevitable that in the coming years both the library and the gallery will be extended to include a wider range of material.

In 2003 the British Museum raised £662,000 to purchase the second-century Roman sculpture known as 'Jennings' Dog'. Contributions from the Heritage Lottery Fund, the National Art Collections Fund, British Museum Friends, the British Museum Trust Fund, supporters of the Greek and Roman Departments and the discerning public made the purchase possible. The dog has a fascinating history: Henry Constantine Jennings, usually known as 'Dog' Jennings, was a wealthy eccentric who habitually dressed in worn shoes, old clothes and a battered hat that he is said to have worn for thirty years. While travelling in Italy with Lord Mothered, during 1753–56, he found, in what might best be described as a junk shop, the statue of a dog. He recognized its quality and bought it for 400 scudi. By the time the statue had reached his home at Shiplake in Oxford, it had cost him £80. Within a short time his neighbours at

Blenheim had offered him £1,400 for the statue. They, too, appreciated its quality. Even Dr Johnson, not usually noted for his visual acuity, and Boswell discussed it at some length. The statue created a considerable stir among discerning members of society. Johann Joachim Winckelmann, a German archaeologist with a particular interest in Herculaneum, Pompeii and Paestum, admired it. Aristocratic doggy households throughout Britain were regarded as incomplete if they did not contain a cast of the statue. Several casts and copies, most dating from the late nineteenth century survive. A left and right pair in marble recently came on the market priced at £32,000. Eventually, the increasingly impecunious Jennings became obliged to sell the statue. It was bought by Thomas Slingby Duncombe, MP for Hertford, who lived in the Vanbrugh pile at Duncombe Park in Yorkshire.

For reasons that are no longer apparent, Jennings decided that the statue was that of Alcibiades' dog. Alcibiades was an Athenian statesman and soldier, born about 450BC and who died in 404BC. Even Socrates was unable to curb his egotistical ostentation or his propensity for treachery. He fought in the war against Potidea and was expected to command the Sicilian expedition against Sicily in 415BC. However, before the expedition all the statues of Hermes in Athens were defaced. Alcibiades was blamed for the gratuitous vandalism. He thereupon changed sides and helped to create an alliance between Syracuse and Persia and encouraged the Athenians to overthrow their democratic rulers. During his tumultuous career Alcibiades is said to have owned a dog that was much admired. Tales of the dog's heroism include one in which it savaged four or five thieves who were trying to steal its gold collar. The dog seems more likely to have been a guard than a hound, in which case Alcibiades may have mutilated it by amputating

its tail, not to destroy its hunting ability but to draw attention to himself.

There is no evidence that a statue ever commemorated the cruelly treated dog; that which the Jennings' dog is claimed to have been a copy of could have been created at any time during the 600 years after Alcibiades had been assassinated. If it does commemorate his dog surely it would be reasonable to expect it to be docked, but why commemorate a dog that belonged to someone who is remembered for his eccentricity and treachery and who finally fell to an assassin? All that can be said is that it may be a Roman copy of a particularly fine piece of Hellenistic animal sculpture of which few have survived. The statue of Jennings' dog is of a type that undoubtedly existed in early Rome. The three-headed Cerberus is usually depicted as of the type. It is identical in every essential respect to an animal represented in a mosaic uncovered in the ruins of Pompeii. Jennings' dog has a luxurious, complete tail, while the Pompeian dog's tail is only slightly less so. A similar type existed in Sparta, but it was not the only type. One type, which probably had its origins in breeds that came from further east, had a broad, short-muzzled head with pendulous ears. This type was referred to as Molossan and was used for hunting large game. Jennings' dog is of a different type, with a sharp muzzle and prick ears. Not only is it probably not Alcibiades dog but also it probably is not a Molossan either.

Research

The use of dogs to provide knowledge that leads to the development of means by which man's own infirmities may be avoided or alleviated and his welfare improved is not new. Whether or not man is justified in using dogs in this way is a matter that is under continual scrutiny and subjected to heated, though often not enlightening debate. In 2004 the Government established a centre for research into the '3Rs' – replacement of animal use in research, refinement of procedures to minimise suffering and reduction of the number of animals used. The centre will improve the lot of all animals used for testing and in experiments, as well as obviating any possible justification for protests that have a propensity to increase their suffering.

In 1666 Pepys was present at an experiment carried out at Gresham College that involved taking blood from one dog and inserting it into another. 'The first died upon the place, and the other did very well.' And two days later, 'the dog which was filled with another dog's blood at the College is very well, and like to be so as ever, and doubts not its being found of great use to men'. It is interesting to think how many lives have since been saved as a consequence of the routine use of blood transfusions. However, the suffering of these dogs and of numerous others might still be regarded as inexcusable. Not all experiments involve a similar degree of suffering. At the beginning of 2004 the Faculty of Veterinary Science set up an archive, the United Kingdom DNA Companion Animal Archive, to gather, with the permission and co-operation of their owners, DNA samples from companion animals suffering from a range of specific diseases. This archival material will be made available to researchers and will help to identify the causes of complex genetic diseases and so lead to the development of new treatments to eradicate some of these conditions. Many of the genes that give rise to these diseases are common to man and other mammalian species, and so the archive will also aid research into human genetics.

Social

Competitive, intellectual and sporting activities are, in part at least, social. Cruft's is much more than the largest and most famous dog show in the world. It also provides a meeting place for people from many countries who share a common interest in dogs in general or in some particular breed or activity. It is a marketplace for the sale of products, both useful and frivolous, for dog owners and also focuses attention on canine art, with exhibitions and sales mounted by major international art houses.

Collecting

Almost every dog owner will find that, after a while, he or she has accumulated all sorts of material about the chosen breed or about dogs in general. This often develops into a serious interest in extending and improving the collection into art works, books, carved sticks and umbrella handles, commercial ephemera, figurines, porcelain and statues of all sizes and ranging in age from thousands of years ago to the present. General outlets for antiques have not yet appreciated what some of this material may be worth to avid collectors and so it is still possible to assemble a collection without remorgaging the family home. Collecting is both an extension of an interest in dogs and a way of acquiring specialized knowledge.

14 Closure

A good man will take care of his horses and dogs, not only while they are young, but when old and past service. ... Many have shown particular marks of regard in burying the dogs which they had cherished and been fond of; and, among the rest, Xanthippus, of old, whose dog swam by the side of his galley to Salamis, when the Athenians were forced to abandon their city, was afterwards buried by his master upon a promontory, which to this day is called the Dog's Grave. We certainly ought not to treat living creatures like shoes or household goods, which, when worn out with use, we throw away, and were it only to learn benevolence to humankind, we should be merciful to other creatures.

Plutarch, *Symposiaca* (AD100)

Attempts to compare the age of a dog with that of a man tend to ignore the difference in the way in which each develops. Dogs, even of breeds about the size of a Fox Terrier, grow more quickly than does a human baby. Every breed also develops into independent creatures in a matter of just a few weeks, whereas our own offspring take years before they can be regarded as independent. The differences between the two species are enormous, but two events, birth and death, are directly comparable.

The Loss of a Pet

All but a few, exceptional owners have been reticent about expressing their grief following the loss of their companion and it is only within the last ten or twenty years that the significance of the loss has come to be appreciated. It is now recognized that losing a dog is, in terms of the sadness and anguish it arouses, not so very different from losing a human friend. The loss may have a more profound effect on the way in which the bereaved owner's life continues. Much has been written about the process of coming to terms with the loss of a much-loved pet. The pet may have been with its owner for several years and have become an integral part of his life. The loss should never be underestimated, especially when it involves the loss of what may be the owner's sole, constant companion.

A bereaved owner may have to face guilt, whether justified or not, may feel that his own life has lost purpose and meaning. He may have to come to terms with grief at the loss of the way in which his life has become the poorer, at the loss of companionship and unconditional love. Nor are such deep feelings confined to the owners of companion animals. During the 2001 foot-and-mouth pandemic some farmers were driven to suicide by the loss of their farm stock. The owners of sporting and working dogs also have to face grief, often commemorated by headstones in the kennel precincts.

Even though there may be no humane alternative to euthanasia, the owner may feel guilt both at the decision itself and at the feelings of grief produced by the loss of an animal. Having a healthy dog put down may also impose a burden on the owner and on a properly sensitive vet. The vet will struggle to deal with an act that runs counter to training and purpose, and the owner may find it difficult to justify the decision. The owner may be moving to a home in which the dog would create problems, she may have or be about to have a child, the pattern of employment may have changed, the dog may be destructive or in some way have become unreasonably demanding. The cost of treating a sick dog, as well as the problem of providing nursing care and the trauma associated with it, may be something that some owners feel unable to face. Canny vets learn to recognize the truth from a reason that is nothing more than a flimsy cover for a desire to trade in a dog for new model, of boarding it while the family is on holiday or a desire to protect a new home or car.

If a healthy dog is to be discarded for good or bad reasons there are other ways of dealing with the problem than killing it. Some national welfare agencies boast that they never put down a healthy dog; others seem to do so without compunction and have a poor record of finding new homes for unwanted dogs, especially for those a mature years. The kindest way to proceed is, in the first place, to consider the breed. All caring breeders will readily help to find new homes for the dogs they have bred. The majority of breeds also have access to a rescue scheme that often has a list of people who are besot-

ted by the breed and are prepared to provide a dog that has fallen on hard times with a new, caring and knowledgeable home. The breed rescue organizations seldom receive the co-operation they deserve from national bodies but they are by far the most efficient means of finding a new home for the breed in which they have a particular interest.

The Ageing Process

Old age is – given good health and a freedom from accidents – inevitable, progressive and irreversible. It is vastly preferable to the alternative. Only among people is it ever suggested, let alone believed, that a cosmetic cream, a simple injection or the cosmetic surgeon's knife can reverse ageing. A survey carried out in 1998 by Andrew Edney examined the reasons for dogs being put down. The survey was conducted among general veterinary practitioners and so excluded the many hundreds of dogs put to death by welfare organizations. Old age or senility and terminal illness accounted for 87 per cent of the dogs destroyed, trauma accounted for almost 5 per cent, 5 per cent had behavioural problems and just over 2 per cent were healthy animals. It is possible that many healthy dogs are consigned to animal shelters where those with intractable behavioural problems may be destroyed. The survey's findings differ significantly from earlier studies that had suggested that approximately 25 per cent were disposed of or abandoned as a consequence of behavioural problems (Bailey, 1992) and that, of the dogs waiting to be rehomed in an animal sanctuary, 33 per cent were said to have behavioural problems. The difference may reflect an improvement in behaviour or improved understanding on the part of owners, or may simply suggest that dogs with behavioural problems are more likely to be abandoned than to be put down by their owners.

Of course, to care for a dog restricts its owner's freedom. At times it may be a nuisance but the benefits usually far outweigh the drawbacks. What other creature will give you such an effusive welcome when you return home from even the briefest trip to the shops? What other creature will be ready at any time to join you in sharing your enjoyment of so many activities?

Most dogs manage the process of ageing with dignity. They may become less energetic but still enjoy playing. They may sleep a lot and more soundly than when they were full of vigour. Hearing and eyesight may deteriorate, but their powers of smell seem to survive intact and will often compensate for the loss of other senses. Like our own species, old age is often accompanied by an increase in irascibility. They may become incontinent, but the effects of previous training remain influential and they should be encouraged to relieve themselves in an appropriate place.

As dogs age they will become less active and so will expend less energy. This should be reflected in their diet; a reduction in the amount eaten, a lower calorific value and an increase in good quality, low-fat protein is called for.

When an aged dog is nearing the end its quality of life will decline in a number of ways. A caring owner will do his utmost to ensure that its diet is appropriate to a failing digestive system, that exercise is gentle but not entirely absent, that incontinence, failing sight and hearing and other troublesome conditions associated with old age are treated sympathetically.

Alzheimer's Disease

A diet that allows scientists to teach old dogs new tricks has been developed in America, raising the prospect that healthy eating could protect the human brain against Alzheimer's disease and other mental signs of ageing. When nine-year-old beagles – deemed to be in late canine middle age – were fed a cocktail of dietary supplements, they showed significant improvement in a mental agility test in which performance usually dips sharply with age.

The findings, from a study led by Carl Cotman, of the University of California at Irvine, suggest that extra antioxidant compounds in the diet protect brain cells against damage from ageing of a sort known as 'oxidative stress'. Cells that would normally die, making the dogs slower and more easily confused, survive and thrive, keeping the brain alert and active. If the cocktail has similar effects on human beings it could potentially be used to help to stave off Alzheimer's and other forms of dementia and age-related cognitive decline, Cotman told the American Alzheimer Association. The beagles in the experiment were given supplements of vitamins C and E, along with alpha lipoic acid, acetyl carnitine, fruit and vegetables. Oranges, kiwi fruit and broccoli are good sources of vitamin C; vitamin E can be found in chick peas, sweet potatoes and avocados; lipoic acid is found in spinach, liver and brewer's yeast, while acetyl carnitine is in red meat, chicken, white fish and milk. The same combination, the ingredients of which are generally available in health food shops, was used two years ago by Bruce Ames, of the University of California at Berkeley, to rejuvenate ageing rats.

In Cotman's test about seventy dogs were trained to pick the odd one out of a collection of objects and were rewarded with food if they did so correctly. Animals aged three normally perform much better than animals aged nine, but the dietary regime almost completely eliminated any difference between the two groups. 'What we found is that we can basically improve learning and memory in these ageing animals so that they can do much more complicated tasks and make many fewer mistakes', Cotman said,

'The data really startled us. The control [animals] continued to get worse and the other animals [on the diet] actually got better than even the beginning baseline performance.'

While dogs do not suffer specifically from Alzheimer's disease, there were encouraging indications from the study that the diet may help to protect against the condition in human beings. The brains of dogs on the diet had lower accumulations of a protein called beta-amyloid, which builds up into sticky plaques in Alzheimer's patients.

Euthanasia

Then years ago she split the air
To seize what she could spy;
Tonight she bumps against a chair,
Betrayed by milky eye.
She seems to pant, Time up, time up!
My little dog must die,
And lie in dust with Hector's pup;
So, presently, must I.

Ogden Nash, 'For a Good Dog'
(*The Private Dining Room*, 1953)

At some stage the owner may have to face the possibility that the dog's quality of life may no longer be of an acceptable quality. At this stage a sympathetic vet will either recommend treatment or help the owner to accept the inevitable fact that the kindest thing is to relieve the dog of its suffering by euthanasia. The principal reasons for this in England are set out below:

Reason	Percentage
Old age or senility	59.6
Terminal illness	27.4
Trauma	4.8
Behavioural problems	5.9
Healthy animal	2.3

(A.T.B. Edney, 'Reasons for the euthanasia of dogs', *Vet. Rec.*, 25 July 1998)

Younger vets may regard euthanasia as an admission of failure, but those who fully appreciate the relationship that exists between an owner and her elderly companion realize that to accept the inevitable can be a valuable welfare tool to alleviate suffering. The situation is a difficult one for both vet and owner. Sometimes it may be necessary for life to be prolonged for a short time to enable the owner to adjust to and accept the inevitable. A good vet will spend time helping the owner to come to terms with the situation. He will do so, not just on the basis of a professional diagnosis but also on the owner's need to come to terms with the imminent event. The owner should not be encouraged to agree to treatment that has little hope of success. Nor should owners be pressed to part with a treasured companion until they have accepted the inevitable. The skills required to manage such a situation are not within the competence of every vet but the best are willing to take time and show the degree of understanding and sympathy required to ease the loss.

The facility to end suffering by means of a simple injection is a final service that we can provide for our dogs, but not for our own species whose suffering cannot be alleviated when body and mind have declined to the point at which nothing is left to make life bearable let alone enjoyable. If we were to subject our pets to similar treatment we would, and should, be prosecuted for cruelty.

Most vets are prepared to visit a dog in its own home so that in its last hours it will not have to endure the stress of a journey or to meet its end in unfamiliar surroundings. The service is one that caring owners appreciate.

Euthanasia usually involves a massive dose of a powerful anaesthetic that immediately puts the dog to sleep and leads to cardiac arrest. Death incurs no pain and, properly managed, little stress for the dog.

Burial

> Now thou art dead, no eye shall ever see,
> For shape or service, Spaniell like to thee.
> This shall my love doe, give thy sad death
> one
> Teare, that deserves of me a million.
> Robert Herrick, 'Upon His Spaniell Trace'
> (*Hesperides*, 1648)

Cynics may pour scorn on the very idea of an owner providing an old friend with a suitable place in death and perhaps to mark that place in some appropriate manner. It is, however, necessary only to remember Robert Herrick, Dr John Arbuthnot, Alexander Pope, Lord John Hervey, Baron Thomas Erskine, Horace Walpole, John Wilkes, William Cowper, Sydney Smith, Richard Barham, Thomas Carlyle and, of course, Lord Byron to realize that doing so is neither new nor mawkish. A stroll round the dog cemetery in Hyde Park will further reinforce the feeling.

Disposing of the remains is perhaps best done by burial in a secluded part of the garden. Quite often a quiet corner can be found for the dog's final resting place and the place marked by a tree or shrub. To dispose of a dog's body in this way is frowned upon by some local authorities, but none has yet been so utterly crass as to prosecute an owner for burying the body of a dog on his own land. Other possibilities include cremation, followed either by unmarked disposal by the vet or at a commercially-run pet cemetery. The choice depends on the owner's wishes and the facilities available. Vets will dispose of the body of a dog if its owner so wishes or is unable to do so for himself. These services incur a cost and are to some degree impersonal, consigning the dog's remains to an unknown fate or a place with which it was not familiar.

Organ Transplants

Veterinary science has developed to the point at which organ transplants are technically feasible. Indeed, the early experimental work on organ transplantation in our own species was carried out on dogs. The number of human lives that have subsequently been saved or significantly improved is incalculable. The problem is an ethical rather than a technical one: donor dogs cannot give their consent to use their organs for transplantation and it would certainly be unethical for a vet to kill dogs in order to harvest organs for use as transplants. The only possible source would be dogs that have been fatally injured in accidents, but the logistics of matching available organs with known need is more complicated than in our own species because, not only do all the same problems apply, but the relative size of donor and recipient must also be matched. Even so, there will undoubtedly be owners who will seek to prolong the life of their dog and in order to do so will ignore ethical considerations and spend considerable sums of money to achieve their purpose.

Appendix I
The Kennel Club General Code of Ethics

1. Owners will properly house, feed, water and exercise all dogs under their care and arrange for appropriate veterinary attention if and when required.
2. Owners will not allow any of their dogs to roam at large or to cause a nuisance to neighbours or those carrying out official duties.
3. Owners will ensure that their dogs will wear properly tagged collars and shall be kept fully leashed or under effective control when away from home.
4. Owners will clean up after their dogs in public places or anywhere their dogs are being exhibited.
5. Owners will agree without reservation that any veterinary surgeon performing an operation on any of their dogs which alters the natural conformation of the animal may report such operation to the Kennel Club.
6. Owners agree not to breed from a bitch in any way which is deleterious to the bitch or the breed.
7. Owners agree only to sell dogs where there is reasonable expectation of a happy and healthy life and will help with the re-homing of a dog if the initial circumstances change.
8. Owners will supply written details of all dietary requirements and give guidance concerning responsible ownership when placing dogs in a new home.
9. Owners will not sell any dog to commercial dog wholesalers, retail pet dealers or directly or indirectly allow dogs to be given as a prize or donation in a competition of any kind.
10. Owners will not knowingly misrepresent the characteristics of the breed nor falsely advertise dogs nor mislead any person regarding the quality of a dog.
11. Owners will ensure that all relevant Kennel Club documents are provided to the new owner when selling or transferring a dog.

Appendix II
Summary of Kennel Club Registrations for All Groups, 2002 and 2003

Group	2002	2003
Hound	11,036	11,679
Gun dog	83,944	93,451
Terrier	36,911	38,960
Sporting breed total	*131,891*	*144,090*
Utility	21,151	23,694
Working	27,206	30,279
Pastoral	23,293	24,031
Toys	22,777	23,800
Non-sporting breed total	*94,427*	*101,804*
Grand total	226,318	245,894

Hound Group	2002	2003
Afghan Hound	214	264
Azawakh (Imp)	0	1
Basenji	72	32
Basset Bleu de Gascogne	7	0
Basset Fauve de Bretagne	63	68
Basset Griffon Vendeen (Grand)	144	97
Basset Griffon Vendeen (Petit)	214	166
Basset Hound	991	1,169
Bavarian Mountain Hound	1	1
Beagle	1,007	1,300
Bloodhound	80	112
Borzoi	107	138
Cirneco Dell'Etna	0	6
Dachshund (Long-Haired)	187	189
Dachshund (Miniature Long-Haired)	1,347	1,359
Dachshund (Miniature Smooth-Haired)	1,102	1,270
Dachshund (Miniature Wire-Haired)	715	693
Dachshund (Smooth-Haired)	216	175
Dachshund (Wire-Haired)	357	310
Deerhound	231	232

Group	2002	2003
Finnish Spitz	29	29
Foxhound	7	13
Grand Bleu de Gascogne	0	3
Greyhound	24	84
Hamiltonstovare	23	28
Ibizan Hound	13	6
Irish Wolfhound	507	437
Norwegian Elkhound	149	122
Norwegian Lundehund	0	0
Otterhound	54	31
Pharaoh Hound	14	13
Portuguese Pondengo	0	35
Rhodesian Ridgeback	1,128	1,255
Saluki	204	85
Segugio Italiano	0	2
Sloughi	6	8
Whippet	1,823	1,946
Total	*11,036*	*11,679*

Pastoral Group	2002	2003
Anatolian Shepherd Dog	46	79
Australian Cattle Dog	42	67
Australian Shepherd	84	84
Bearded Collie	901	668
Belgian Shepherd Dog (Groenendael)	73	93
Belgian Shepherd Dog (Laekenois)	1	5
Belgian Shepherd Dog (Malinois)	55	59
Belgian Shepherd Dog (Tervueren)	220	150
Bergamasco	0	0
Border Collie	2,113	2,111
Briard	159	209
Collie (Rough)	1,492	1,377
Collie (Smooth)	85	77
Estrela Mountain Dog	51	21
Finnish Lapphund	17	42

Group	2002	2003
German Shepherd Dog		
(Alsatian)	14,177	14,892
Hungarian Kuvasz	0	0
Hungarian Puli	78	83
Komondor	0	11
Lancashire Heeler	125	208
Maremma Sheepdog	22	17
Norwegian Buhund	34	42
Old English Sheepdog	620	729
Polish Lowland		
Sheepdog	68	35
Pyrenean Mountain		
Dog	209	213
Pyrenean Sheepdog	7	35
Samoyed	523	367
Shetland Sheepdog	1,500	1,684
Swedish Lapphund	0	0
Swedish Vallhund	17	40
Welsh Corgi (Cardigan)	56	74
Welsh Corgi (Pembroke)	518	559
Total	*23,293*	*24,031*

Terrier Group	**2002**	**2003**
Airedale Terrier	1,054	855
Australian Terrier	34	38
Bedlington Terrier	338	403
Border Terrier	5,339	6,447
Bull Terrier	2,665	2,924
Bull Terrier (Miniature)	278	234
Cairn Terrier	1,664	1,605
Cesky Terrier	22	13
Dandie Dinmont		
Terrier	148	90
Fox Terrier (Smooth)	167	226
Fox Terrier (Wire)	665	593
Glen of Imaal Terrier	48	26
Irish Terrier	198	303
Kerry Blue Terrier	244	283
Lakeland Terrier	269	213
Manchester Terrier	86	122
Norfolk Terrier	494	472
Norwich Terrier	153	143
Parson Russell Terrier	673	969
Scottish Terrier	982	1,055
Sealyham Terrier	58	60
Skye Terrier	59	67
Soft-Coated Wheaten		
Terrier	277	352
Staffordshire Bull Terrier	10,711	11,325
Welsh Terrier	270	319
West Highland White		
Terrier	10,015	9,823
Total	*36,911*	*8,960*

Group	2002	2003
Toy Group	**2002**	**2003**
Affenpinscher	119	196
Australian Silky Terrier	23	8
Bichon Frise	2,225	2,142
Bolognese	36	60
Cavalier King Charles		
Spaniel	9,984	10,614
Chihuahua (Long Coat)	865	878
Chihuahua (Smooth		
Coat)	373	440
Chinese Crested	399	397
Coton de Tulear	21	29
English Toy Terrier		
(Black and Tan)	56	88
Griffon Bruxellois	141	192
Havanese	37	81
Italian Greyhound	105	92
Japanese Chin	197	227
King Charles Spaniel	150	176
Lowchen (Little Lion		
Dog)	116	122
Maltese	396	381
Miniature Pinscher	181	170
Papillon	642	708
Pekingese	720	682
Pomeranian	664	652
Pug	1,105	1,392
Yorkshire Terrier	4,222	4,073
Total	*22,777*	*23,800*

Working Group	**2002**	**2003**
Alaskan Malamute	238	341
Beauceron	17	26
Bernese Mountain Dog	769	839
Bouvier des Flandres	103	126
Boxer	8,916	9,542
Bullmastiff	1,831	1,768
Canadian Eskimo Dog	0	8
Dobermann	2,706	3,171
Dogue de Bordeaux	797	1,238
German Pinscher	20	20
Giant Schnauzer	258	259
Great Dane	1,736	1,892
Greenland Dog	6	14
Hovawart	14	33
Leonberger	371	315
Mastiff	408	580
Neapolitan Mastiff	333	317
Newfoundland	930	978
Portuguese Water Dog	38	67
Pyrenean Mastiff	1	4
Rottweiler	5,802	6,369

Group	2002	2003
Russian Black Terrier	69	91
Siberian Husky	985	1,491
St Bernard	821	762
Tibetan Mastiff	44	28
Total	*27,213*	*30,279*

Utility Group	2002	2003
Akita	1,311	1,593
Boston Terrier	184	213
Bulldog	1,936	2,270
Canaan Dog	26	19
Chow Chow	407	424
Dalmatian	2,071	2,253
Eurasier	0	9
French Bulldog	247	349
German Spitz (Klein)	77	144
German Spitz (Mittel)	85	130
Japanese Shiba Inu	163	128
Japanese Spitz	115	87
Keeshond	88	77
Lhasa Apso	3,065	3,344
Mexican Hairless	5	0
Miniature Schnauzer	2,607	2,873
Poodle (Miniature)	741	897
Poodle (Standard)	976	1,116
Poodle (Toy)	1,172	1,354
Schipperke	100	104
Schnauzer	372	383
Shar-Pei	1,040	1,220
Shih Tzu	3,113	3,343
Tibetan Spaniel	254	275
Tibetan Terrier	996	1,089
Total	*21,151*	*23,694*

Gundog Group	2002	2003
Bracco Italiano	15	23
Brittany	98	105
English Setter	568	577
German Long-Haired Pointer	13	18

Group	2002	2003
German Short-Haired Pointer	1,348	1,406
German Wire-Haired Pointer	396	413
Gordon Setter	250	399
Hungarian Vizsla	731	773
Hungarian Wire-Haired Vizsla	72	157
Irish Red and White Setter	99	123
Irish Setter	1,225	1,293
Italian Spinone	379	325
Kooikerhondje	7	2
Lagotto Romagnolo	19	34
Large Munsterlander	153	147
Pointer	657	858
Retriever (Chesapeake Bay)	152	128
Retriever (Curly Coated)	79	125
Retriever (Flat Coated)	1,296	1,353
Retriever (Golden)	10,526	10,710
Retriever (Labrador)	35,996	41,306
Retriever (Nova Scotia Duck Tolling)	82	91
Slovakian Rough-Haired Pointer	5	19
Spaniel (American Cocker)	503	549
Spaniel (Clumber)	170	134
Spaniel (Cocker)	13,417	14,832
Spaniel (English Springer)	12,431	13,884
Spaniel (Field)	84	75
Spaniel (Irish Water)	145	121
Spaniel (Sussex)	82	68
Spaniel (Welsh Springer)	437	362
Spanish Water Dog	37	70
Weimaraner	2,472	2,978
Total	*83,944*	*93,458*

Useful Contacts

The Animal Health Trust, Lanwades Park, Kentford, Newmarket, Suffolk, CB8 7UU

Association of Pet Behaviour Counsellors, PO Box 46, Worcester WR8 9YS

Association of Pet Dog Trainers, Peacocks Farm, Northchapel, Petworth, West Sussex, GU28 9JB

British Dog Groomers Association, Bedford Business Centre, 170 Mile Road, Bedford, MK42 9TW

British Small Animals Veterinary Association (BSAVA), Woodrow House, 1 Telford Way, Waterwells Business Park, Quedgeley, Glos. GL2 4AB

Countryside Alliance, 367 Kennington Road, London SE11 4PT

Defence Animal Centre (DAC) Document Procurement Section, Welby Lane, Melton Mowbray, Leics., LE13 0SL

Department of Environment, Food and Rural Affairs, Events & Audiovisual, Room 221, 10 Whitehall Place, London SW1A 2H

Federation Cynologique Internationale, Place Albert, 1er 13, B-6530 Thuin, Belgium

Guide Dogs for the Blind Association, Hillfields, Burghfield Common, Reading, Berks., RG7 3YG

Hearing Dogs for Deaf People, The Grange, Wycom Road, Saunderton, Bucks, HP27 9NS

HM Customs and Excise, 5th Floor East, New Kings Beam House, 22 Upper Ground, London, SE1 9PJ

International Sheepdog Society, Clifton House, 4a Goldington Road, Bedford, MK40 3NF

Irish Kennel Club, Fottrell House, Unit 36, Greenmount Office Park, Dublin 6W

The Kennel Club, 1–5 Clarges Street, Piccadilly, London, w1J 8AB

Pet Advisory Committee, 1 Bedford Ave., London, WC1B 3AU

Pet Bereavement Support Service (PBSS), The Blue Cross, Burford, Oxfordshire, OX18 4PF

Pet Care Trust, Bedford Business Park, 170 Mile Road, Bedford, MK42 9TW

PRO Dogs National Charity & Pets as Therapy, Rocky Bank, 4 New Road, Ditton, Kent, ME20 6AD

Society for Companion Animal Studies (SCAS), The Blue Cross, Burford, Oxfordshire, OX18 4PF

Bibliography

For owners who want to know more about their chosen breed, activities that interest them, the history of dogs or their place in art or literature or in society at large, there are numerous books that deserve to be read (there are also a great many that offer little of value or interest). For anyone with an interest in breeding or who is just curious about what breeders are doing, there is no better source than the Kennel Club's Breed Record Supplement, published quarterly in sections devoted to each of the groups. The BRS records the names of the owners who had bred a litter during the period, the name of the sire and the bitch, plus details, dates when any previous litters and the number of puppies produced by the bitch and the number and registered names of puppies in the litter and their colour.

What follows is no more than a small selection of the books that will also repay study:

Cummins, John, *The Hound and the Hawk, The Art of Medieval Hunting* (Weidenfeld & Nicholson, 1988)

Darwin, Charles, *The Expression of the Emotions in Man and Animals* (1872)

Fox, Michael W., *Understanding Your Dog* (Blond & Briggs, 1972)

Gaita, Raimond, *The Philosopher's Dog* (Routledge, 2002)

Ireson, Peter, *Another Pair of Eyes, The Story of Guide Dogs in Britain* (Pelham Books, 1991)

Jackson, Frank (ed.), *Faithful Friends, Dogs in Life and Literature* (Robinson, 1997)

Jackson, Frank, *Dog Breeding* (The Crowood Press, 2000)

Kellert, Stephen R. and Wilson, Edward O., *The Biophilia Hypothesis* (Island Press, 1993)

Lorenz, Konrad, *Man Meets Dog* (Methuen, 1954)

Lorenz, Konrad, *On Aggression* (Methuen, 1963)

Morris, Desmond, *Dogs, A Dictionary of Dog Breeds* (Ebury Press, 2001)

Serpell, James, *In the Company of Animals* (Blackwell, 1986)

Serpell, James (ed.), *The Domestic Dog: Its Evolution, Behaviour and Interactions with People* (Cambridge University Press, 1995)

Thomas, Keith, *Man and the Natural World Changing Attitudes in England 1500–1800* (Penguin Books, 1983)

Trumler, Eberhard, *Understanding your Dog* (Faber & Faber, 1973)

Turner, Trevor, *Veterinary Notes for Dog Owners* (Popular Dog, 1990)

Waugh, Evelyn, *The Loved One* (Penguin Books, 1948).

Index